Weird, Wacky and Wild

PENNSYLVANIA TRIVIA

D1600531

Weird, Wacky and Wild

PENNSYLVANIA TRIVIA

Jodi M. Webb & Lisa Wojna
Illustrations by Roger Garcia, Peter
Tyler, Patrick Hénaff & Pat Bidwell

BLUE
BIKE
BOOKS

The Publisher: Blue Bike Books
Website: www.bluebikebooks.com

Library and Archives Canada Cataloguing in Publication

Webb, Jodi M., 1969–   Pennsylvania trivia : weird, wacky & wild / Jodi
Webb & Lisa Wojna.

ISBN 13: 978-1-897278-40-6
ISBN 10: 1-897278-40-3

   1. Pennsylvania—Miscellanea. I. Wojna, Lisa, 1962– II. Title.

F149.5.W43 2008   974.8   C2008-903900-9

Project Director: Nicholle Carrière
Project Editor: Wendy Pirk
Production: Alexander Luthor
Cover Image: © Tony Spuria | Dreamstime.com
Illustrations: Roger Garcia, Peter Tyler, Patrick Hénaff, Pat Bidwell

We acknowledge the support of the Alberta Foundation for the Arts for our
publishing program.

PC: 01

DEDICATION

For Beth, Jeanette and Nathan, who had to listen to random stories about Pennsylvania during supper.

–JMW

CONTENTS

ACKNOWLEDGMENTS

To everyone at Blue Bike, including my co-author Lisa Wojna.

So many people contributed to my writing this book that it seems impossible to thank everyone, but I'm going to give it a shot anyway. First, for everyone who made creating this book so easy for me by telling me their stories or making me a part of their lives. You made me want to write a book about what makes Pennsylvania home.

For Sister Pacelli, who lit the flame by suggesting that I might be able to make a living by writing, and Dr. Bill Gudelunas, who told coal cracker stories in history class even though only he and I laughed.

A million thanks to Matt Holliday and *Pennsylvania Magazine* for publishing my first article and teaching me a lot about Pennsylvania through the years.

Thanks to the Black Diamond Writers Group, who celebrated this book as if it was their own, especially Sara.

And to John—who has been building me bookshelves and fanning the flame for 18 years.

–JMW

Many thanks to our clever editor, Wendy, who pieced together the work of two authors and did so seamlessly, to my co-author, Jodi, and to my family—my husband Garry, sons Peter, Matthew and Nathan, daughter Melissa and granddaughter Jada. Without you, all this and anything else I do in my life would be meaningless.

–LW

INTRODUCTION

Pennsylvania has many commendable qualities—natural beauty, exciting cities, friendly people—but what sets it apart from the other 49 states is its history. I know what you're thinking: "Hmmph, history. Every state over a day old has history." True, but nobody has history quite like Pennsylvania. Our history isn't just dusty old displays that school kids visit on field trips to museums. Pennsylvania history isn't just for people from Pennsylvania—our state history is the history of every American citizen.

Quick, ask somebody who isn't from the state to name a few historical events, people or things from Pennsylvania. What did they say? Lincoln giving the Gettysburg Address, Washington crossing the Delaware, winter at Valley Forge, July 4 and the Declaration of Independence, Benjamin Franklin flying his kite…anyone who passed fifth grade history can tell you how Pennsylvania contributed to our nation's history. But we don't just leave history to school books and historical societies. Want to walk through the streets, the houses, the places where history was made? Chances are, in our state they still exist—just as they did decades or centuries ago.

In Pennsylvania, history is more than just dates from history books. You can find history in the places we live. Go to the small towns and you can see how history lives from generation to generation. Stop someone on the street and ask if anyone famous lived there or how the town got its name. In Pennsylvania we know. We'll tell you about the life of James Buchanan, stops along the Underground Railroad or Cornelia Bryce Pinchot's fight for social justice. As you float down the Susquehanna or Schuylkill River or visit Catawissa or Tamaqua, you almost expect to see the Native American who named them just around the next corner. A host of towns' names reflect other countries—the places settlers first called home: Avon, Hamburg, New Holland. Our town museums, festivals or even just simple displays at the local library celebrate our town's history.

For us, history is personal. It's not just the accomplishments of politicians and soldiers—we value each person and the role he or she played in history. A visit deep underground in the cool, dark silence of the Pioneer Mining Tunnel in Ashland can tell a visitor more about our ancestors' lives than a hundred books about anthracite coal mining. But not all our history is solely in the past—for many it's still a big part of their everyday lives.

As next door neighbors to several coastal states, Pennsylvania became home to thousands of immigrants who tired of the crowded cities that greeted many of them "just off the boat." Even though they were proud to be Americans and Pennsylvanians, our immigrant ancestors still upheld their traditions. Peek into many Pennsylvania homes (especially around the holidays) and you will witness history—we still speak the words of our ancestors, enjoy the ethnic songs and dances, and cook our *gnocchi*, pepper cabbage and *pierogies* with recipes scribbled generations ago by *nonnas, omas* and *babcias*. Perhaps the best example of Pennsylvanians preserving their ancestors' way of life is the Amish people who live apart from the modern world with their old-fashioned clothes, buggy transportation and one-room schoolhouses.

Is there a word for people who live history? Of course—Pennsylvanians!

THE NAME GAME

What's in a Name?

In 1681 when King Charles II granted him a tract of land in what is now Lancaster County, William Penn set about establishing a safe haven for Quakers and other religious groups facing persecution in their homeland. The only proviso given to Penn was to send the king two beaver pelts each year, and to name the area Pennsylvania—"Penn" after its original settler and *sylvania*, which is the Latin word for "woodlands." Pennsylvania was almost automatically nicknamed "Penn's woods."

Also Known As

Pennsylvania, like any other state, has its fair share of nicknames. Perhaps the most commonly used nickname is the Keystone State. How did it get this name? Well, there are a few theories. The word "keystone" is defined by Merriam-Webster as "the wedge-shaped piece at the crown of an arch that locks the other pieces in place," and Pennsylvania sits in an interlocking position to the neighboring states of New York, New Jersey, Maryland, West Virginia and Ohio. Or, the name may be a reference to Pennsylvania's vote for independence, which supposedly was passed by a single, "keystone" vote. Another explanation for the moniker was the fact that the state's initials, PA, were carved into the keystone of the arch that supports the Pennsylvania Avenue Bridge. In any case, the first documented use of the term "keystone" in reference to Pennsylvania was in 1802 when, during a victory rally for the newly elected President Thomas Jefferson, the state was called "the keystone of the federal union."

Other nicknames:

☛ The Quaker State for the Quakers who originally settled in the area (not originally for Quaker State oil, though that comes later).

☛ The Oil State for the oil industry, one of the state's economic backbones.

☛ The Coal State for Pennsylvania's coal mining industry.

☛ The Steel State for yet another major Pennsylvanian industry.

Making it Official

William Penn may have arrived and named Pennsylvania back in 1681, but it didn't become a state until December 12, 1787. It was the second state admitted to the Union, acquiring that status just five days after Delaware became the first state in the newly forming nation.

Pennsylvania Peculiarities

You're called a Pennsylvanian if you come from the Keystone State. You are also a member of a commonwealth—Pennsylvania, Virginia, Kentucky and Massachusetts are the only four states in the nation to hold the designation of commonwealth and state. Both terms are used when referring to these states.

DID YOU  KNOW?

The United States Mint began issuing specially designed state quarters in 1999, and Pennsylvania was the second state to receive one. More than 5300 ideas for the coin's design were submitted. The winning suggestion sports the statue of "commonwealth," which tops the state capitol building, overlaid on the outline of the state. The coin also contains a keystone and the words "Virtue, Liberty, Independence."

SYMBOLS OF THE STATE

Coat of Arms

Long before there was officially a state of Pennsylvania, there was a Pennsylvania Coat of Arms—or at least the rudimentary beginnings of one. In 1778, Philadelphia resident Caleb Lowens created the design, very similar to what we know today—two horses on either side of a crest that bears the images of a ship, a plowshare and wheat stalks, topped with an American Bald Eagle and underscored by an olive branch, a cornstalk and the state motto. Originally there was a corn stalk behind each horse, but those were removed in the 1805-revamped design. Other changes were made throughout the years until a final version was decided upon in 1875. Strangely enough, even after a series of changes, this final design is almost identical to the original one created by Lownes.

Although not used in the same kind of official capacity as the state seal, Pennsylvania's Coat of Arms is considered the State's best-known symbol.

State Seal

The General Assembly of Pennsylvania adopted an official state seal in 1791. The central images of the ship, plowshare, sheaves of wheat, eagle and corn stalks featured on the crest of the Coat of Arms are displayed prominently in the center of the face side of the seal, surrounded by the words "Seal of the State of Pennsylvania." This is the most frequently used portion of the seal, but the reverse side also bears a symbol and message. Also known as the "counterseal," the image is of a wand-bearing woman (representing liberty) conquering a lion (representing tyranny). This design is bordered by the phrase, "Both Can't Survive."

Flying High

It's really no wonder why Pennsylvania's Coat of Arms is considered the state's most recognizable symbol—it appears in various forms on the state seal and the state flag. Passed by an Act of the General Assembly on June 13, 1907, Pennsylvania's official flag bears the Coat of Arms front and center on a royal blue background that is bordered in gold. The only difference between this version and the original 1799 version is the standardization of the flag's blue background.

Other State Symbols

☛ On October 2, 1959, an act of the general assembly of the Pennsylvania Legislature made it official—the white-tailed deer *(Odocoileus virginianus)* was named the state animal.

☛ They might do things big down in Texas, but there's little doubt as to which state boasts the largest state dog designation. That honor was captured by Pennsylvania, hands down, as soon as it adopted the Great Dane *(Canis familiaris),* William Penn's favorite breed, as the official state dog on August 15, 1965. It's known as the Barking Vote because the legislators signaled their approval with a series of arfs, yips and woofs.

☛ The eastern hemlock *(Tsuga Canadensis Linnaeus)* was named the state's official tree in 1931.

☛ Although Pennsylvania doesn't have an official state bird, it does distinguish the ruffed grouse *(Bonasa umbellus)* as its official state game bird. It was adopted as such by an act of legislature on June 22, 1931.

☛ Got milk? If you do, you're not only downing a healthy drink, you're celebrating Pennsylvania's state beverage. It was so named on April 29, 1982.

☛ The mountain laurel *(Kalmia latifolia)* was designated Pennsylvania's official state flower in 1933, but it wasn't the first choice for the position. In 1927, the snow-white flowers so distinctive of the tulip tree *(Liriodendron tulipifera L.)*, and the tree itself were submitted for consideration for official state flower and tree, respectively. Although the suggestion garnered a lot of discussion—both in support of and against the motion—no decision was made. In 1931, the question of an official state flower was raised again, this time with the pink azalea and the mountain laurel vying for the honor. It was another two years before the matter was finally settled—Governor Gifford Pinchot apparently asked his wife to make the final decision, and though he preferred the pink azalea, the mountain laurel emerged as victor.

☞ All you avid anglers out there might be interested to know that the official state fish of Pennsylvania is the brook trout *(Salvelinius fontinalis)*. It received the designation on March 9, 1970.

☞ The delicate Penngift Crownvetch *(Coronilla varia L. Penngift)*, which grows so prolifically throughout Pennsylvania, was named the state's official "beautification and conservation plant" in 1982.

☞ In 1987, Pennsylvania named an official state electric loco-motive. The lucky winner of that nomination was the GG1 4859 Electric Locomotive, which made its first journey to Harrisburg in January of 1938. If you want to check it out, you'll have to travel to that city and visit its Transportation Center. A total of 139 GG1-model locomotives were made from the 1930s until the early 1980s.

☞ The General Assembly also named an official state steam engine in 1987. The K4s Steam Locomotive captured that honor.

☞ Pennsylvania's concern for preserving the state's nature was reinforced, once again, in 1988 with the naming of an offi-cial state arboretum—the Morris Arboretum and Gardens of the University of Pennsylvania. The center boasts some of the state's largest, oldest and rarest trees.

☞ On May 26, 1988, the General Assembly named the newly restored United States Brig Niagara as Pennsylvania's state flagship. It's on display on the shores of Lake Erie, which is fitting seeing as the ship was a key player in the Battle of Lake Erie in 1813.

☞ Also in 1988, the trilobite *(Phacops rana)* was named the state's official fossil.

☞ Just like the beloved Tinkerbell, the firefly has captured the imagination of youngsters everywhere. On April 10, 1974, the luminescent insect was chosen as the official state insect. However, on December 5, 1988, the General Assembly took that designation a step further and named a specific species of firefly, Poturis Pensylvanica De Geer, as the state insect.

☞ The Philly Pops orchestra has been around since 1979, entertaining Pennsylvanians with the best in "popular classics and new favorites," and in 1999 they were rewarded for their efforts when they were named the state's official pops orchestra.

☞ Proudly perched on the corner of 9th Avenue and Walnut Street is the country's oldest theatre. The Walnut Street Theatre was founded in 1809, initially as a venue for equestrian acts under the name The New Circus, and has continued to awe audiences every season, without fail. In 1999, the General Assembly recognized this longstanding commitment to the arts in Pennsylvania by naming it the state's official theatre.

Motto
Pennsylvania's official motto is "Virtue, Liberty and Independence." I think that says it all, don't you?

Singing Our Praises!

Pennsylvania's state song, conveniently called "Pennsylvania"—written by Eddi Khoury and put to music by Ronnie Bonner—was given its official status on November 29, 1990.

Unfortunately, not many Pennsylvanians were aware of the song, something the state's legislature was hoping to rectify.

So on November 20, 2007, Rep. Merle Phillips, Rep. Russ Fairchild and 39 of their colleagues passed a resolution declaring November 25 to 30 of that year as "Sing Pennsylvania Week." To make their point loud and clear, as it were, they invited 26 members of the Winfield Baptist Church Chorale to belt out their own memorable rendition of the state song right there on the House floor. Along with impressing the members of the House, the performance was televised live on PCN TV. I've included the lyrics below, just in case you wanted to commit them to memory. As you read through, I'm sure you'll agree it's a lovely song indeed.

"Pennsylvania"

Verse 1
Pennsylvania, Pennsylvania,
Mighty is your name,
Steeped in glory and tradition
Object of acclaim.
Where brave men fought the foe of freedom,
Tyranny decried,
'Til the bell of independence
Filled the countryside.

Chorus
Pennsylvania, Pennsylvania,
May your future be,
Filled with honor everlasting
As your history.

Verse 2
Pennsylvania, Pennsylvania,
Blessed by God's own hand,
Birthplace of a mighty nation,
Keystone of the land.
Where first our country's flag unfolded,
Freedom to proclaim,
May the voices of tomorrow
Glorify your name.

CLIMATE & WEATHER

A Mixed Bag

Pennsylvania is a land with a varied landscape. Mountain ranges and lush farmland make this a beautiful state with no end of natural attractions. Its topography also affects its climate. Although the state is said to lie in a "humid continental zone," changes in elevation affect everything from the average temperatures experienced throughout the year to the amounts of precipitation you can expect to see in any given location. Warm to moderate, crop-friendly temperatures are common in the Ohio and Monongahela valleys to the southwest and southeast respectively, as well as the part of Pennsylvania bordering Lake Erie. Cooler temperatures are the norm for higher elevations. And though some sources might suggest Pennsylvania can expect an average summer temperature around 70°F and an average winter temperature at around 30°F, others will point out that it's impossible to narrow down averages so precisely because the geographic factors of the state are so varied it has five temperature zones.

A Look at the Averages Across the Board

☛ Average July temperatures in the 74°F and higher mark can be expected in the southeast portion of Pennsylvania, surrounding the cities of Philadelphia, Allentown and Harrisburg.

☛ Summer temperatures below the 68°F mark are generally the norm in the north-central portion of the state.

☛ Overall, Pennsylvania typically experiences cold winters. Generally the same north-central portion of the state with the lowest average summer temperatures can expect winter temperatures below the 22°F mark.

☞ Again, the southern part of the state experiences less severe winter conditions, with average January temperatures bottoming out around 28°F.

☞ Central Pennsylvania and the areas along the state's western border are usually its driest sections, with an average of less than 40 inches of precipitation falling in any given year.

☞ Small pockets of the state, such as a long, narrow strip of land west and north of Allentown can expect more than 48 inches of precipitation per year.

Brrrr…C-C-C-Cold!

On January 5, 1904, Smethport recorded the state's lowest-ever temperature. It was a frigid −42°F that day.

Hot, Hot, Hot

The highest temperature ever recorded in Pennsylvania was 111°F. The hotspot that scored that record, which was set on July 10, 1936, was Phoenixville.

Biggest Downpour

It rained for 24 hours straight, on July 24, 1942, dumping 34.5 inches of rain at Smethport—the largest amount of rainfall in a single 24-hour period to date.

Worst of the Worst

Johnstown. Just mention the name and most folks in Pennsylvania will have heard of the place, largely because of the rapid snowmelt or extreme rainstorms that have led to at least three major floods of note—in 1889, 1936 and 1977.

The first, and perhaps most deadly and destructive, of the three disasters took place on May 31, 1889. Residents were buckling down in the upper stories of their family homes, preparing to wait out the worst of the storm on higher ground, as it were, when the unthinkable happened. The South Fork dam, located about 14 miles from Johnstown and, admittedly, in a rather questionable state of disrepair, gave away. In that instant, the waters of Lake Conemaugh, which the dam held back, were unleashed. According to accounts of the disaster from the

Johnstown Flood Museum, "within the hour, a body of water, which engineers at the time estimated moved into the valley with the force of Niagara Falls, rolled into Johnstown with 14 miles of accumulated debris, which included horses, barns, animals and people, dead and alive."

The aftermath of this flood was almost cataclysmic in scale. A total of 2209 people died. That number included 99 entire families. The Plot of the Unknown in Grandview Cemetery holds the remains of 750 victims who were never identified, and the fact that bodies were still being discovered as late as 1911 is like something out of a horror flick. About $17 million in property damage was reported, and the debris covered 30 acres of land.

Three days of rain and a quick snowmelt led to the flood disaster of March 17, 1936. Photos of Johnstown during that flood show streets submerged under 5 or 6 feet of water in some places, businesses destroyed and infrastructure ruined. About two dozen people died in the flood, 77 buildings were completely destroyed, and accumulated property damage was believed to be around $41 million.

They say bad luck comes in threes, and this certainly was the case when it came to Johnstown's unfortunate experience with floods. On July 20, 1977, the community was devastated yet again as floodwaters claimed 85 lives and caused $300 million in property damages.

Hurricane Force

The most deadly, damaging storm to hit Pennsylvania was Hurricane Agnes. The storm started out as a tropical disturbance on June 14, 1972, and made its way from the Yucatan Peninsula along the Florida panhandle and into Georgia and the Carolinas, gaining strength as it traveled. By the time it reached north-central Pennsylvania, it had calmed a bit, but it soon let out its full fury. In the end, Pennsylvania reported the greatest amount of property damage ($2,119,269,000) and the highest number of deaths (48) of any state. By comparison, New York was the state hit second hardest, and it reported 24 deaths and $702,502,000 in property damages. Although Hurricane Agnes was only rated as a Category 1 hurricane when it was over Florida, the sheer volume of the rain that fell made Agnes more than twice as destructive as any other hurricane that has hit the U.S.

Winter's Fury

Summer storms in Pennsylvania have been deadly and destructive, but that doesn't mean winter storms haven't caused havoc as well. In fact, a blizzard that raged from March 12 to 15, 1993, is usually touted as the "storm of the century." Tornado-force winds were reported throughout the country's eastern seaboard, bringing uncharacteristically cool temperatures and large amounts of precipitation—for example, Pittsburgh reported a two-foot snowfall.

PENNSYLVANIAN GEOGRAPHY

Size Matters

Good things come in small packages, and though Pennsylvania is far from the country's smallest state, it ranks 33rd when it comes to size. Rectangular in shape, Pennsylvania measures 283 miles from its eastern to western borders and 160 miles from its south and north borders. Altogether, the state covers a total area of 46,058 square miles, 2.7 percent (or 1239 square miles) of which is covered by water.

The Lay of the Land

Pennsylvania, considered a mid-Atlantic state, acts as a divider that separates the most northerly states of the Atlantic seaboard from the southern ones. Pennsylvania is bordered by New York to the north and New Jersey to the east. Delaware is nestled against the most easterly portion of Pennsylvania's southern border, Maryland against the central portion and West Virginia borders the southwestern corner of the state. Ohio is located directly west. The southeasterly portion of the state, near Philadelphia and Chester, is nestled along the Delaware River near the Delaware Bay, and the northwesterly portion of the state borders Lake Erie, so despite the fact that Pennsylvania is surrounded by land, it is definitely not landlocked.

High Point
At 3213 feet in elevation, the summit of Mount Davis is the highest point in Pennsylvania.

Middle Ground
Overall, the state's average elevation is 1100 feet.

Low Point
Because Pennsylvania touches the Delaware River, which empties into the Atlantic Ocean, it should be no surprise that the state's lowest elevation is measured at sea level.

Front and Center

If you drive 2.5 miles southwest of Bellefonte, you'll find yourself at a longitude of 77°44.8'W and a latitude of 40°53.8'N or, in other words, smack dab in the center of the state. It's no coincidence, then, that Bellefonte is located in Centre County.

Major Lakes

Pennsylvania is known for a lot of things, not the least of which is the state's natural beauty, but it isn't home to a whole lot of lakes large enough to warrant much attention. In fact, the only lake that sources list as a major lake isn't solely the property of Pennsylvania—it's shared with New York, Ohio, Michigan and Canada. In case you haven't figured it out by now, that lake is Lake Erie. It's certainly earned the title of "major lake" as the 10th largest lake in the world, covering an area of 9940 square miles. The average depth of Lake Erie is 62 feet, which makes it the shallowest of the five Great Lakes. The largest lake totally within the borders of the state is the 8300-acre Raystown Lake, constructed by the U.S. Army Corps of Engineers primarily for flood control. At 200 acres, the largest natural lake within the borders is Conneaut Lake, west of Meadsville.

Major Rivers

There are 45,000 miles worth of rivers and streams in Pennsylvania. The major rivers contributing the most to that length of waterway are the Allegheny (which starts out at Raymond and meanders along for about 325 miles); the Delaware (which borders Pennsylvania and New York and extends 360 miles); the Susquehanna River (which at a length of 444 miles is the longest river on the east coast and ranks 16th longest in the country); and the Ohio (which, though it extends for 981 miles into the Midwest, begins in Pittsburgh, is sourced by the Allegheny and meanders all the way to Cairo, Illinois).

Pennsylvania's Earthquake History

Early accounts of earthquakes affecting the state of Pennsylvania are vague. Formal records of such occurrences weren't established until 1737, when the first settlement in the area was founded, but even then details were sketchy. Here are some details of the more prominent earth-shaking events:

☛ On December 18, 1737, an earthquake stretching from Delaware to New York toppled chimneys in a number of communities, including Philadelphia.

☛ Philadelphia reported severe earthquakes on March 17 and November 29, 1800.

☛ Philadelphia-area earthquakes on November 11 and 14, 1840, caused swells on the Delaware River.

☛ An earthquake reported in New York City on May 31, 1884, caused structural damage and sent dishes flying off the dinner table as far away as West Chester.

☛ A fairly centralized earthquake with an intensity of 6 on the Richter scale was reported in Allentown on May 31, 1908. The quake caused some chimneys to tumble, but tremors were only felt in a 58 square mile radius.

☞ Dishes flew off tables and out of cupboards in kitchens across Erie after an earthquake with an intensity of 5 on the Richter Scale struck the area on October 29, 1934. Several other earthquake shocks caused similar damage in Sinking Spring on January 7, 1954; Wilkes-Barre on February 21, 1954; Lehigh Valley on September 14, 1961; Philadelphia on December 27, 1961; Cornwall on May 12, 1964; and Philadelphia again on December 10, 1968.

☞ Other relatively minor quakes have occurred since 1968, but the most widespread earthquake experienced in Pennsylvania, measuring 5.2 on the Richter scale, occurred on September 25, 1998. Tremors were felt throughout most of the state and into parts of Ohio, Indiana, Michigan, New York, Virginia and even southern Ontario, Canada, but the only damage reported was some minor upsets to the ground-water system in the Greenville-Jamestown area.

County Curiosities

Pennsylvania is composed of 67 counties, and the name of one—Philadelphia—serves both as a county and a city. Here are a few unique claims to fame for each:

☞ Because we already mentioned it, let's start with Philadelphia. Located in southeastern Pennsylvania, Philadelphia County was established in 1682 and was one of the state's three founding counties. It occupies a total area of 143 square miles. The county seat is the city of Philadelphia, and the business of the county and city were combined in 1854, though their respective offices didn't merge until 1952. The name "Philadelphia" is a Greek term that roughly translates as "brotherly love."

☞ Adams County, one of Pennsylvania's southern border counties, was founded in 1800. The county prides itself on its fruit industry and its historical contributions to the American Civil War.

☛ The English translation for the Lenape name "Allegheny" is unclear. The county was founded in 1788 and named after the Allegheny River. There must be something in the water there that inspires the artistic mind, because several notables hail from the area, including actors Michael Keaton and Jeff Goldblum, artists Mary Cassatt and Andy Warhol, songwriter Stephen Collins Foster, pianist and composer Ethelbert Nevin and director George Romero.

☛ Parts of Allegheny, Westmoreland and Lycoming counties were annexed in the forming of Armstrong County in 1800.

☛ Mapmakers plotting Beaver County must have liked even numbers. The county itself is comprised of 444 square miles, with 10 square miles of that being water and the remaining 434 square miles being land.

☛ Along with being mighty proud of its natural beauty, the folks down in Bedford County are pretty excited about the 14 covered bridges located within their boundaries. According to their visitors' bureau, these bridges were hand built about 100 years ago, and the skill of their craftsmanship is evident in the fact that they're still around and as roadworthy as ever.

☛ Berks County was founded on March 11, 1752, and named after Berkshire, England, William Penn's hometown.

☛ The ladies generally outnumber the men in Blair County. According to the 2000 Census, there were 100 females to every 88.5 males aged 18 and older.

☛ Bradford County was originally settled as Ontario County on February 21, 1810. It was restructured and renamed Bradford County two years later, after William Bradford, a Pennsylvania Supreme Court Justice and United States Attorney General.

☛ Another of Pennsylvania's three founding counties, Bucks County was officially established in November of 1682. Folks there are proud of their roots, and not only does the county have its own seal and flag, it also has a number of county symbols. Buck County boasts an official flower (the violet), bird (the cardinal), mammal (cotton tail rabbit), tree (dogwood), fish (catfish) and rock (diabase). Students from grades three to nine chose the symbols back in the 1980s.

☛ Butler County calls its lush, beautiful landscape a "playground for all ages." The county also advertises its homegrown produce with the logo, "You Can't Buy Better Than Butler" and provides an opportunity for residents and visitors alike to support locals by purchasing gift baskets stuffed with everything from Butler County honey to potatoes, maple syrup, onions, spaghetti sauce and more—you might want to keep this in mind when you're doing your Christmas shopping.

☛ Although much smaller population-wise than Cambria County's largest city, Johnstown (population 23,906), Ebensburg is the home of the county's seat. There are only 3091 folks living in Ebensburg, according to the 2000 Census. The city's central location was likely one of the factors that led to its being named the county seat.

☛ Cameron County's logo boasts about its landscape, loud and clear: Land of Endless Mountains.

☛ Founded on March 13, 1843, Carbon County was named for the large amounts of coal deposits found in the region. The harvested coal was transported by rail, which is likely one of the reasons why Carbon County calls itself "home of the first railroad in America that was built on any large scale."

☛ Centre County, founded on February 13, 1800, was so named because it's front and center, geographically speaking of course.

☛ One of Pennsylvania's three founding counties, Chester County was founded in 1682. In 2004, the Census estimate placed the county's population at around 465,795 people, making it the state's seventh most populated county. It's also, according to some sources, considered Pennsylvania's wealthiest county.

☛ Clarion County and its town seat, Clarion, were both named after the Clarion River. This county was founded on March 11, 1839. One of its many claims to fame, according to the county website, is that Clarion is home to one of "the most important tracts of virgin timber" in the state.

☛ Clearfield County was also named after a waterway—Clearfield Creek. The name was likely adopted because of the "clear fields," or large tracts of open land thought to be a result of herds of bison roaming the area in its early history.

☛ Clinton County is home to five Pennsylvania state parks: Bucktail State Park Natural Area, Hyner Run State Park, Hyner View State Park, Kettle Creek State Park and Ravensburg State Park.

☛ The poetic name Columbia was originally used to refer to the entire country, referencing Christopher Columbus, and Columbia County was named with that in mind.

☛ As of the 2000 Census, 90,366 people inhabited the 35 townships, 14 boroughs and two major cities that make up Crawford County.

☛ If you look at per capita income levels, Cumberland County ranks as the fifth wealthiest county in Pennsylvania. It's per capita income, according to the census, was $31,627.

☛ Dauphin County can trace its name back to French roots. When it was formed in 1785, it was named after Louis XVI's first son, Louis-Joseph Dauphin of France. The title of "Dauphin" meant he was France's heir apparent. Folks from that corner of the state call it the sweetest place on the earth to live.

☛ Covering an area of 191 square miles, Delaware is one of Pennsylvania's smaller counties. Population-wise, however, it's pretty dense, with 550,864 residents calling it home, according to the 2000 Census. That's equal to a population density of almost 2900 people per square mile.

☛ If you wonder what kind of wildlife you might encounter when traveling through Elk County, just think of its name. Although the population of elk might not be as prolific as it once was, you'll likely still catch a glimpse or two of the magnificent creatures.

☛ As its name suggests, Erie County is located along the shores of the Great Lake of the same name. Its county seat is the town of Erie, home to such cultural icons as the Erie Philharmonic, the Erie Playhouse and the Lake Erie Ballet.

☛ Fayette County is nothing if not historic. It's home to 15 historic districts, 48 historic markers, five national historic landmarks, two national parks and more than 50 historic buildings and sites—not to mention it's also the home of Jim Delligatti. In case you need a reminder, Delligatti is the guy who invented the Big Mac and birthed the mega franchise McDonald's.

☛ With a 2000 population of 4946, Forest County is the state's least populated county. The total land area is 431 square miles, making the county's population density slightly more than 11 people per square mile.

☛ Of course, Franklin County was named after Benjamin Franklin. It was founded on September 9, 1784.

☛ Greene County's original log courthouse, built in Waynesburg in 1797, is still standing and open to visitors. It was refurbished and rededicated in 2002.

☛ Robert Fulton, an 18th century inventor, was so respected for his invention of what is commonly referred to as the "first commercially successful steam-powered steamboat" that Fulton County was named in his honor.

☛ Disney enthusiasts who enjoyed the 1969 movie featuring the Volkswagen beetle known and loved as Herbie the "Love Bug" might enjoy taking a trip down to Huntingdon County to check out the Swigart Museum. That's where the retired Herbie now makes his home.

☛ Residents in Indiana County quiet literally celebrate Christmas all year long; at least they do when it comes to preparing for the season's annual Christmas tree harvest. The county is known for shipping more than one million Christmas trees to locations across the country, giving it good reason for calling itself the "Christmas Tree Capital of the World."

☛ Punxsutawney Phil, the nation's official Groundhog Day groundhog, is from none other than Punxsutawney, Pennsylvania. In case you weren't aware of the fact, Punxsutawney is located in Jefferson County.

☛ An abundance of white-tailed deer, wild turkey, grouse, bear and other game make Juanita County a haven for avid hunters.

☛ One reason Lancaster County is a big draw for tourists is its large population of Amish residents. Also known as Pennsylvania Dutch, the Amish are a deeply religious Christian order committed to simple living, and they shun modern conveniences such as electricity and telephones. If you're into homespun crafts, there are no better examples of the variety and quality of handmade quilts around—they are what the Pennsylvania Dutch are known for. The Quilt Museum and the Old Country Store in Intercourse are great places to view (and maybe even buy) these beautiful art pieces.

☛ Lebanon County is known for more than it's beautiful landscape and lush farmland. It's also known for its pork production, especially its famous Lebanon Bologna.

☛ Lehigh County boasts more than 11,000 acres worth of preserved farmland—land that is purchased by the Bureau of Agricultural Land Preservation and set aside as an "agricultural conservation easement." The program, initiated because of the rapidly dwindling amount of farmland in the county, raised funds through a number of initiatives, one of which was a two-cent per package tax on the sale of cigarettes. The purchase of lands for preservation purposes began in 2002.

☞ In 1930, Luzerne County reported a population of 445,000 residents, which is the highest number of residents to ever have lived in the county. Since then, the population has continued to decline, and in 2004, population estimates put the number of county residents at 313,431.

☞ The French were the first Europeans to arrive in Lycoming County. In fact, the first European man in the area was one Etienne Brule. He arrived in 1615.

☞ When it comes to being proud of one's heritage, folks in McKean County have a lot to boast about. They've an abundant supply of oil and timber, they're the home of the Zippo lighter, and they call themselves the "Black Cherry Capital of the World."

☞ Mercer County's current courthouse was built in 1909, but it was the county's third courthouse building. The first was erected in 1807 at the same site and went through several changes and additions before it burned down in 1866. The construction of a second courthouse began right away, but that too burned down in December of 1907. So far number three is a charm.

☞ There are about 46,486 people living in Mifflin County, according to the 2000 Census. Of those, 24.6 percent were under the age of 18.

☞ Munroe County was founded in 1836, and in the last 30-plus years, its population has grown so rapidly that it's more than tripled (from 45,422 in 1970 to 138,687 in 2000), making it the second-fastest growing county in the state.

☞ There is such a high concentration of deer in Montgomery County that in January 2008, its Parks and Heritage Services Department conducted a one-day hunt of female deer at the Norristown Farm Park. The decision to host a regulated hunt was based on an effort to save the area's ecosystem, which had been taking a beating from deer grazing.

☞ Covering a total area of 132 square miles, Montour County is the smallest county in the state. It was founded in 1850, and was named after a colonial Indian leader named Madame Montour.

☞ You might not be aware of the fact, if you're not a racecar enthusiast, but Northampton County is home to the Andretti family. Aldo, Michael, Jeff and John all raced professionally, and Marco is still competing in the Indy league.

☞ Coal has been a main industry in Northumberland County for centuries, especially in the Shamokin district. It was first marketed there in 1814.

☞ Oliver Hazard Perry, War of 1812 hero who died around the time Perry County was formed in 1820, was honored in the naming of this county.

☞ Pike County is one of Pennsylvania's most ethically diverse, with 93.10 percent of the population classified as white, 3.2 percent as black or African American, .62 percent as Asian, .24 percent as Native American, .01 percent as Pacific Islander, 1.30 percent from "other races" and 1.47 percent made up of two or more races.

☞ Potter County covers a total area of about 1081 square miles, and virtually none of that is made up of water.

☞ Schuylkill County has eight neighboring counties, beginning with Luzerne County to the north, followed in a clockwise direction by Carbon, Lehigh, Berks, Lebanon, Dauphin, Northumberland and Columbia counties.

☞ Recycling is something the management of Snyder County takes quite seriously—so much so that they've come up with a unique recycling idea. In January, collection bins were set out in post offices, schools, the courthouse and selected businesses so folks could drop off the greeting cards they've collected throughout the year. The program collected more than 1500 pounds of cards for all occasions. Used cards were recycled as drywall backing, and unused cards were sent to the Selinsgrove Center, a seniors' residence.

☛ Somerset County is known for its preponderance of snow. In fact, one source calls it "one of the snowiest inhabited locations in the United States." Some areas of Somerset County have recorded more than 200 inches of snow in a winter, and area folklore has it that in 1816 it even snowed in July. The annals of history now refer to that time as "the year without summer."

☞ The largely rural Sullivan County refers to itself as the "Gem of the Endless Mountains." Aside from natural resources and tourism, the area is home to a thriving arts community that creates and sells everything from hand woven baskets to jewelry and maple syrup.

☞ Joseph Smith translated the Book of Mormon, sometime between 1827 and his death in 1844, while in Susquehanna County. Smith is also credited with founding The Church of Jesus Christ of Latter-day Saints.

☞ Union County has it all. It boasts of being a great place to live, work and visit, and if you're down in that neck of the woods and looking for something to do, just check out the county's website. Folks there are so considerate, they've provided readers with a "Top Ten Things To Do" list—and every item looks worth checking out.

☞ Just about every American youngster has heard of Johnny Appleseed, and many have likely recited the mealtime prayer he's featured in, but I bet most aren't aware of the fact that Johnny Appleseed, born as John Chapman, was once a resident of Venango County.

☞ Eight counties surround Warren County. Starting north and moving in a clockwise direction, they are Chautauqua, Cattaraugus, McKean, Elk, Forest, Venango, Crawford and Erie counties.

☞ Washington County was founded in 1781 and named after George Washington, the first president of the United States. In case you were wondering, Washington served as president from 1789 to 1797.

☞ The first jail built in Wayne County was erected in Bethany in 1801, but the building that really draws the crowds is the Old Stone Jail. Built in Honesdale in 1859, the building welcomed its first criminal even before the jail was officially open. The prisoner was a gent named Thomas Lee, arrested for robbing a Binghamton store. He arrived in June of 1859 and served his sentence amid the chaos of construction until August of the same year, when the jail officially opened its doors.

☛ As far as voting preference goes, it appears the folks in Tioga County tend to vote Republican far more often than people in many of the other counties in the state.

☛ Westmoreland County's first courthouse was actually the res- idence of Robert Hanna and was located at Hannastown. The Hanna house served double duty as a residence and as the place where county business was conducted from the time the county formed on February 26, 1773, until 1786.

☛ According to the 2000 Census, a female headed 9.3 percent of Wyoming County households.

☛ York County is located along Pennsylvania's southeastern border and runs along the Mason-Dixon Line.

DID YOU KNOW?

There are about 55,000 farms occupying 9,000,000 acres worth of farmland in Pennsylvania.

THE ENVIRONMENT

The Big Picture

Of the 46,058 square miles of total area that make up the State of Pennsylvania, 1.4 million acres are State Game Lands.

Pennsylvania Wildlife Overview

According to the folks down at the American Society of Mammalogists (ASM), Pennsylvania is rich in wildlife. There are about 28 mammal species, ranging from the Virginia opossum and the white-tailed deer to the coyote and the red fox, considered common throughout the state. However, there are almost 40 other species whose numbers are rapidly declining and whose status range from uncommon all the way to extinct. Here's a look at some of the more uncommon species and their status according to ASM statistics:

Common Name	Status	Location of Habitation
Rock shrew	Uncommon	Appalachian Uplands
Pygmy shrew	Uncommon	Presumed statewide
Water shrew	Uncommon	Mountain streams
Hairy-tailed mole	Uncommon	Statewide
Eastern mole	Uncommon	Piedmont and Valley Ridge
Star-nosed mole	Uncommon	Statewide
Red bat	Uncommon	Statewide
Hoary bat	Uncommon	Statewide
Silver-haired bat	Uncommon	Statewide
Eastern pipistrelle	Uncommon	Statewide
Fox squirrel	Uncommon	South and West
Southern bog lemming	Uncommon	Statewide
Porcupine	Uncommon	North and Central
Ermine	Uncommon	Most of the state
Black bear	Uncommon	Uplands
Kenn's myotis	Rare	Statewide
Seminole bat	Rare	Piedmont
Evening bat	Rare	Southeast
New England cottontail	Rare	Eastern Mountains
Snowshoe hare	Rare	Appalachian Uplands
Northern flying squirrel	Rare	North
Rock vole	Rare	Northeast
Least weasel	Rare	Western two-thirds of state
Eastern spotted skunk	Rare	South-central
River otter	Rare	North

Common Name	Status	Location of Habitation
Bobcat	Rare	Appalachian Uplands
Small-footed myotis	Threatened	Statewide
Eastern woodrat	Threatened	Mt. Ridges
Least shrew	Endangered	South-central
Indiana bat	Endangered	Central

(Note: The moose, bison, lynx, mountain lion, wolverine, badger, marten and gray wolf, all once known to exist in the wilderness areas of Pennsylvania, are now listed as extinct within state boundaries.)

Cold-Blooded Conservation

The Pennsylvania Biological Survey lists 36 amphibian species and 37 reptile species native to the commonwealth. There are 17 species of frogs and toads and 22 salamanders in the list of Pennsylvania amphibians and 14 turtle, 4 lizard and 21 snake species native to the state.

Lost Forever?

The eastern tiger salamander, midland smooth soft-shell turtle and eastern mud turtle have all been extirpated (their populations have been completely destroyed) from Pennsylvania.

S-S-S-S-S-S-snakes

Of the 21 species of snakes indigenous to Pennsylvania, most are harmless (unless, of course, you're like me—absolutely snake-phobic in which case the mere sight of any variety is enough to induce a myocardial infarction). There are three species, however, that are venomous: the timber rattlesnake, northern copperhead and Eastern Massasauga rattlesnake. Of the three, only the Eastern Massasauga rattlesnake is listed as an endangered species.

A greater percentage of Pennsylvania's non-venomous snakes are in some way threatened. Here's a list of some of the less abundant species and their status:

Common Name	Status
Eastern worm snake	Rare
Eastern kingsnake	Rare
Queen snake	Rare
Shorthead garter snake	Rare
Earth snake	Rare
Rough green snake	Threatened
Kirtland's snake	Endangered

A Little Out of the Ordinary

There's rare—and then there's exotic. Pennsylvania has its share of unique species not indigenous to the area. Among them is the now-thought-to-be-extinct Italian wall lizard, introduced to the area sometime in the early 1900s.

The Erie National Wildlife Refuge is the only national wildlife refuge with populations of the rare clubshell (a type of mussel). The species was once common to the eastern U.S. but is now on the endangered species list.

Keeping an Eye on Things

The Pennsylvania Game Commission was instituted in 1895. The organization is responsible for managing 1.4 million acres of State Game Lands throughout the commonwealth. One particularly demonstrative success story can be seen in the state's black bear population. As recently as the 1970s, the number of black bears in Pennsylvania was estimated to be about 4000—a relatively small number for such a common species. Today that number has more than tripled, with an estimated count in the 14,000 range. Such an increase in numbers means these large animals need to expand their range, and that often brings them into conflict with humans. The Game Commission is responsible for monitoring annual hunts—the 2004 season saw 2972 bears taken. That's the fourth largest bear kill since the state started keeping track in 1915. The commission also lobbies the government to pass laws making it illegal to feed bears, thereby lessening the likelihood of contact, and it maintains a database recording human-bear issues.

DID YOU KNOW?

According to The Pennsylvania Department of Conservation and Natural Resources, "Pennsylvania's rain and snowfall are more acidic than any other region in North America." Some ecologists say acid rain could be responsible for changes in the forest structure and that "forest communities are being increasingly dominated by acid tolerant [plant] species, such as striped and red maple." The metal toxicity resulting from high acid content in streams and waterways also affects water quality for area fish and other wildlife.

Preserving the Land

The Pennsylvania Forestry Association was formed in 1886, responding to the rapid loss of natural lands as the state went through its own industrial revolution of sorts. Natural resources were being targeted at a rapid rate, with more than 30,000 saw-mills popping up throughout the nation by 1870. Pennsylvania's lumber industry was thriving, too, with more than $29 million in annual sales. But that took its toll on the landscape, and pretty soon Pennsylvania was being referred to as the "Pennsylvania Desert." Combining the concern for preserving the states natural environment and history, Governor Robert E. Pattison signed Act 130 in 1893. This legislation enabled the state to acquire the area surrounding Valley Forge. The goal was to transform it into a public park. The action paved the way for the establishment of the state's first state park and helped establish Pennsylvania's state park system. Almost 100 years later, on July 4, 1976, the state gifted the park to the country, and it's now known as Valley Forge National Historical Park. More than 1.2 million people visit the park's 3500 acres each year. In 2007, Pennsylvania boasted 117 state parks covering 2.1 million acres of state game lands. There are also eight natural areas protected by national park status. In addition, both the state and the federal government protect other areas for their historical significance.

It's All in the Name?

Prince Gallitzin State Park, located in the Allegheny Plateau Region of the state, was named after honest-to-goodness royalty. Father Demetrius Augustine Gallitzin, son of Prince Dimitri Alexievitch Gallitzin, Russian Ambassador to Holland, chose the church as his life's calling. He was just 22-years-old when, in 1792, he traveled to the United States. Encouraged by the civil and religious liberty embraced by this new country, Gallitzin decided to devote his life to the church, and after studying at the Sulpician Seminary in Baltimore, he was ordained on March 18, 1795. He became the first person in the United States to be ordained into the priesthood. It wasn't the only credit to his name. Gallitzin went on to establish St. Michael's Parish, the area's first Catholic Church, and he wore many hats, from that of teacher and banker to doctor, lawyer and businessman who'd encouraged the establishing of a gristmill, tannery and sawmill in the community where he served. His dedication and commitment to his new country was recognized with the naming of the Prince Gallitzin State Park, and he's remembered in history as the "Apostle of the Alleghenies."

PA POPULATION

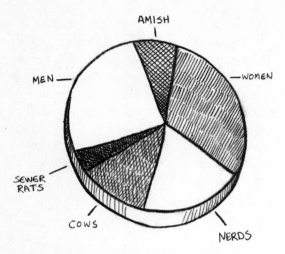

One, Two, Three...

The population of Pennsylvania, based on the 2000 U.S. Census, was 12,281,054 (2006 estimates put that number at closer to 12,440,621) making it the sixth most populated state in the country. Spread that number out over the entire state and that's the equivalent of 274.02 persons per square mile.

Breaking it Down

Generally speaking, the population of Pennsylvania looks something like this:

☛ 5.8 percent are under the age of five

☛ 22.5 percent are under 18

☛ 15.2 percent are 65 or older

☛ 51.4 percent are female

☛ About 4.1 percent of Pennsylvania's residents were born in a country other than the U.S.

☛ 8.4 percent of folks aged five years and older speak a language other than English at home.

☛ 81.9 percent of people aged 25 and older are high school graduates, bettering the national average by 1.5 percent.

☛ 24.4 percent of those 25 and older have earned a Bachelor's degree or higher, again bettering the national average of 22.4 percent.

☛ Of the population aged five and older, 2,111,771 people struggle with some type of disability.

Population by Ancestry

The five most prominent ethnic backgrounds in Pennsylvania are:

☛ German at 27.66 percent of the population

☛ Irish at 17.66 percent

☛ Italian at 12.82 percent

☛ English at 8.89 percent

☛ Polish at 7.23 percent

Ethnic Diversity

The following statistics are based on 2006 estimates from the U.S. Census Bureau.

Race	Percentage of Population
White	85.7
White (non-Hispanic)	82.1
Black	10.7
Hispanic or Latino	4.2
Asian	2.4
Persons with two or more racial backgrounds	1.0
American Indian and Alaska Native	0.2

The Top 10

Harrisburg might be the capital city of Pennsylvania, but it's far from the state's largest city. In fact, it doesn't even make it on the top 10 list. Counting down from the top spot, here are Pennsylvania's most populated cities, based on 2000 Census figures:

City	Population
Philadelphia	1,517,550
Pittsburgh	334,563
Allentown	106,632
Erie	103,717
Upper Darby	81,821
Reading	81,207
Scranton	76,415
Bethlehem	71,329
Lower Merion	59,850
Bensalem	58,434

County Countdown

Counting down from the top spot, here are Pennsylvania's most populated counties, based on 2000 Census figures:

County	Population
Philadelphia	1,517,550
Allegheny	1,281,666
Montgomery	750,097
Bucks	597,635
Delaware	550,864
Lancaster	470,658
Chester	433,501
York	381,751
Berks	373,638
Westmoreland	369,993

Small but Proud

The county with the smallest population is Forest County. According to the 2000 Census, 4946 residents called that county home.

DID YOU KNOW?

According to the 2006 U.S. Census Bureau estimates, despite the fact that Philadelphia's population is thought to have decreased from 2000 figures of 1,517,550 to 1,448,396, it still ranks as the country's sixth most populated city.

Pennsylvania's Population Through the Years

Census Year	Population Figure
1790	434,373
1800	602,365
1820	1,049,458
1840	1,724,033
1860	2,906,215
1880	4,282,891
1900	6,302,115
1950	10,498,012
2000	12,281,054

(based on U.S. Census figures)

DID YOU  KNOW?

As with many other states in the nation, the largest 10-year increase in population, percentage-wise, in Pennsylvania occurred during its founding years. Between 1790 and 1800 the population grew by 34.5 percent, or by 167,952 persons. The largest influx of people during a 10-year period was recorded between 1900 and 1910 when the population grew by more than 1.3 million, from 6,302,115 to 7,665,111.

Middle of the Road

The average age of Pennsylvania residents, according the U.S. Census 2000 figures, is 38 years. The largest population group falls in the 35 to 44 category with 1,948,076 or 15.9 percent of the population.

Golden Years

On average, Pennsylvanians can expect to live well into their 70s. The county boasting the highest life expectancy is Centre County at 79.4 years and the county with the lowest life expectancy is Philadelphia at 72.3 years.

The Name Game

According to the Pennsylvania Department of Health, the five most popular names chosen by parents of baby girls in 2005 were Emily, Madison, Emma, Olivia and Abigail with 896, 869, 859, 792 and 729 girls given those names respectively. Michael, Jacob, Matthew, Ryan and Nicholas rounded off the top five boy name picks by new parents with 1102, 1000, 989, 963 and 937 baby boys receiving those names respectively.

 In 2007, Pennsylvania ranked as the 23rd healthiest state in which to live, up from the 29th spot in 2006. It slipped a little to 33rd ranking in the most livable state category in 2007, down from the 30th position in 2006. But where Pennsylvania really shines is when it comes to ranking the brainiest states. In 2006–07 it ranked in 10th spot, albeit a slip from 9th in 2004–05.

Ranking Number One

According to the Pennsylvania Visitors Network, the state ranks first in the entire nation when it comes to the following categories: "rural population, number of licensed hunters, State Game Lands, covered bridges, potato chip production, pretzel bakeries, licensed bakeries, meat packing plants, and mushroom, sausage and scrapple production." (In case you were wondering, and I certainly was, scrapple is defined as "a mush of ground pork and cornmeal that is set in a mold and then sliced and fried.")

Religious Preferences

With a nickname like "The Quaker State" and many resident still strongly tied to their immigrant roots (including the church of their ancestors), it's no surprise that Pennsylvania is considered a fairly religious state. Of the 12,281,054 residents, almost 8.5 million reported being a member of an organized religion. The Association of Religion Data Archives at Pennsylvania State University has logged information on 7,116,348 of those individuals. Here's a breakdown on a few of the more popular religious and denominational preferences, based on 2000 Census figures:

Christian Denomination/ Religion	Number of Participants
Roman Catholic	3,802,524
United Methodist Church	659,350
Evangelical Lutheran Church	611,913
Presbyterian Church	324,714
Jewish (estimate)	283,000
United Church of Christ	241,844
American Baptist	132,858
Episcopal Church	116,511
Assemblies of God	84,153
Muslim (estimate)	71,190
Amish (estimate)	39,000

ROADSIDE ATTRACTIONS

A Daredevil's Delight

I wouldn't go on a roller coaster under the best of circumstances, so I'm not the least bit tempted by Leap-The-Dips at Lakemont Park in Altoona. But for thrill-ride aficionados, this roller coaster is something you've simply got to try. Leap-The Dips is the oldest, continually operating "slide friction" wooden roller coaster in the world. The 1452-foot-long ride is shaped in a figure eight pattern, reaches heights of 41 feet off the ground and was built by Edward Joy Morris in 1902. Over the years, it's had its difficulties, and in 1999 it had to be rebuilt, but it continues to tempt visitors to try out its 10 miles-per-hour thrill.

Horse Lovers Alert!

If you're one of those people who salivates at the thought of horses, plan a visit to the Land of Little Horses Farm Park, at 125 Glennwood Drive, Gettysburg. And when they say "little," they aren't joking. The park is home to miniature horses, most of which are 28" to 34" tall. The farm offers hands-on activities introducing visitors to park animals, an in-depth history of the park and its pets, harness races, children's pony rides and more. Check ahead before you stop by, though, because hours change depending on the season.

One Big Collection

As a kid, I collected stamps. Then there was the spoon collection phase—they were all the rage a couple of decades ago. Books are definitely my biggest downfall now. And I have friends who collect assorted animals—pigs and cats and, yes, even elephants. But Ed Gotwalt puts them to shame. He

received his first elephant as a wedding gift—a token for good luck—and it triggered a lifetime of collecting. His elephant collection now numbers more than 6000. He opened a museum in 1975, and the admission price is a very affordable one—it's free! Once there, you'll see elephants of all shapes and sizes, from PEZ dispensers, plush toys and ornamental clocks to an elephant potty chair. Some elephants are made of wood or plastic and others are made from more exotic materials—one elephant is even pulling a circus wagon made of 24-karat gold. The aptly named "Mister Ed's Elephant Museum" is located at 6019 Chambersburg Road in Orrtanna. If you're in the neighborhood, stop by. As their motto promises, "You'll Never Forget... Mister Ed's Elephant Museum."

Philadelphia, The Story

If you're the kind of person who's more drawn to urban settings, the city of Philadelphia is a must-visit destination. Three very distinctive neighborhoods with three very different histories share one square mile, spanning the area between Front and 7th streets and Spruce and Race streets. Trendy shops are often housed in historic buildings, museums recount state and national history, you can visit familiar national symbols such as the Liberty Bell and the nightlife is to die for.

Fantasy Wilderness

Eeeerie, spookie, smelly—but alluring none-the-less, the Indian Echo Caverns, near Hershey-Humelstown, offers visitors the very best in spelunking experiences. Indian Echo Caverns promises a "learning and educational" experience that takes about 45 minutes to tour. Visitors can expect to see all the typical stalactites, stalagmites and other underground formations created by moisture and the flow of minerals. The tour takes visitors through varied passageways and "rooms," including the "Indian ballroom" and the "wedding chapel." The caverns have been open to the public since the 1920s. Before that, from 1802 until 1821, it was considered the home of the "Pennsylvania Hermit," William (Amos) Wilson.

An Unexpected Pagoda

A pagoda would be right at home in any city, but Reading's Pagoda isn't in Chinatown—there is no Chinatown. Instead, this town's pagoda is in an old stone quarry on Mount Penn. Well, it was a stone quarry until the neighbors started complaining to owner William Abbot Witman Sr. that he was turning a beautiful picnic spot into one ugly mountaintop. No longer able to stand his neighbors' angry looks, Witman closed the quarry. But what was he going to do with the 10 acres of Mount Penn he still owned?

Witman found the answer in an unlikely place—a postcard of the Japanese fortress, Nayoga Castle. His friend architect Charles C. Matz got to work, and by 1908, Berks County could look up on the mountain and see its own little bit of Japan. The seven-storey hotel had five red tile roofs, a 175-year-old bell straight from Japan (via the Suez Canal), a golden dolphin, and devils' heads on the corners to frighten away evil spirits. Apparently the devils' heads didn't frighten the city administrators—they decided not to give the hotel an alcohol license. Who would after seeing the winding dirt road that customers would have to navigate down the mountain after a few drinks at the Pagoda's restaurant? Jonathon Mould bought the pagoda two years later but couldn't figure out what to do with a pink pagoda that had no alcohol license. He sold it to the city for $1 to use as a park.

In the years before radios became popular, the pagoda brought the news to residents of Berks County, with a little help from local newspapers. When sporting events or elections were being held, the newspapers would publish Pagoda codes in their morning issues. In the evening, residents of Berks County could watch flashing lights on the pagoda's tower to learn up-to-the-minute results. World War II blacked out the pagoda and it was largely forgotten until 1969 when city leaders decided to tear it down. The citizens protested and the Pagoda was saved—not only saved from the wrecking ball but adopted as the city's most famous (and weirdly out of place) landmark. Although folks now get their election results from CNN, the pagoda became a cultural center for art exhibits, concerts and other community events. And you can still look up each evening and see the neon glow of the pagoda on the mountaintop.

YOU'VE GOT TO SEE THIS

Ringing Loud and Clear

The Liberty Bell is a must-see for folks living in or visiting Pennsylvania—if you're anywhere in the state, you simply must tour the Liberty Bell Center in Philadelphia. Within the simple copper and tin-cast bell are hundreds of years of tradition and history.

The story of the Liberty Bell is as convoluted and complex as the history of the founding of any country. The first bell was cast in Britain's Whitechapel Foundry in 1752 and was delivered for installation at Independence Hall (then known as the Pennsylvania State House) in 1753. The 2080-pound bell was created from a mix of 70 percent copper, 25 percent tin and trivial amounts of lead, zinc, arsenic, gold and silver, and though it was thought to be able to withstand the work of any bell of its kind, a crack appeared. One urban legend suggests the crack appeared at the bell's first ringing, and another suggests the bell was dropped from the temporary scaffolding it was hanging from. However, a member of the State Assembly, Isaac Norris, wrote "...it was cracked by a stroke of the clapper without any other viollence[sic] as it was hung..." In any case, like the mirror in Alfred Lord Tennyson's poem "The Lady of Shalott," the bell was cracked from top to bottom and needed replacing. Instead of sending the bell all the way back to England, legislators turned to two local foundry workers—John Pass and John Stow—to melt down and recast the bell. The Pass and Stow version was rejected because its sound was "unpleasant," so Pass and Stow gave it another try. Their second effort didn't pass muster either, so a new bell was ordered from Whitechapel in 1754. It arrived later that same year and was hung in the State House cupola. The Pass and Stow bell remained in the steeple and, for a time, both bells were rung for different events. Here are a few more interesting Liberty Bell trivia bits:

☛ "Pennsylvania" is misspelled on the Liberty Bell as "Pensylvania". Or is it? At the time the bell was cast, the spelling of the state's name hadn't been standardized, so one "n" didn't look out of place. Now it screams "forgot to spell-check."

☛ The original bell was referred to as the "State House Bell." After it was recast, it was referred to as the "Pass and Stow bell." It wasn't called the "Liberty Bell" until the abolitionist movement began calling it that in 1837. Other replicas included the Centennial Bell, gifted to Philadelphia in 1876, and the Bicentennial Bell, gifted to the entire country by Queen Elizabeth II on her 1976 visit to Philadelphia.

☛ Worried the British would capture Philadelphia during the revolution and melt down the Liberty Bell for ammunition, the Army announced that the bell had been sunk in the Delaware River. In reality it was moved to Allentown in October 1777, where it was hidden under the floor of the Old Zion Reformed Church for nine months.

☛ The first incarnation of the Liberty Bell wasn't the only one to crack. A hairline crack was noted on the Pass and Stow recast version in 1835 (probably the result of tolling for Supreme Court Chief Justice John Marshall), and then in 1846 a much larger zigzag crack was noted (most likely from ringing the bell in honor of George Washington's birthday).

☛ The 24.5 inch long and .5 inch wide "crack" in the Liberty Bell that visitors see today is actually repair work done on it in 1846. The work, called "stop drilling," was meant to prevent reverberations from making the crack bigger. The actual crack is just a hairline crack—though it is approximately 28 inches long.

☛ More than 1.5 million people visit the Liberty Bell each year.

☛ In April of 2001, 26-year-old Mitchell Guilliatt attacked the bell with a hand sledge while taking part in a visitor's tour.

☛ On October 9, 2003, the Liberty Bell Center—now home to the Pass and Stow bell—opened in the Historic District of Philadelphia. From the center, visitors can see the bell's first home—Independence Hall.

One-of-a-kind Museum

If you're the kind of person who enjoys road trips, you might want to take in a unique museum experience. The Lincoln Highway Heritage Corridor (LHHC) is one of 12 designated heritage areas in the state. It's located along the Lincoln Highway and follows along a portion of the first coast-to-coast highway in the country. As it wends its way throughout the roughly 200 miles from its easternmost point in Pennsylvania to the state's western border, the LHHC passes through six counties—Westmoreland, Somerset, Bedford, Fulton, Franklin and Adams. About 75 interpretive exhibits highlighting the state's history and culture have been set up along the route, and travelers are encouraged to stop and take in as many of these roadside "museum" experiences as possible.

The entire highway stretches for 3389 miles from New York to San Francisco and was finished in 1925.

Planes in Pennsylvania

In Pennsylvania, if you want to climb a mountain, you don't always have to get out your hiking boots. The state has the country's most operational inclined planes or funicular railways (taken from the Latin word *funis* for "rope"). These unusual railways have two tracks running parallel to each other, with one car on each track. The cars are attached to each other with steel cables and pulleys. They move simultaneously: when one car comes down the mountain, its weight pulls the other car up.

Monongahela Incline (1870)—the Pittsburgh railway is the oldest continuously operating inclined plane.

Duquesne Incline (1877)—this Pittsburgh incline was saved from being shut down in 1963 by the Society for the Preservation of the Duquesne Incline.

Johnstown Inclined Plane (1891)—with a 70.9 percent incline, it is the world's steepest. During the Johnstown floods, residents used the incline to reach higher ground.

Altoona Funicular (1992)—was built so tourists could view the Altoona Horseshoe Curve without having to climb the 194 steps to the observation platform.

Remembering Yesterday

By the time you're a couple of decades old, you can look back and recognize how things have changed. Consider the 20th century, for example, and how many advancements in technology have occurred and changed how we live our lives. Visitors to Chester County might want to check out one of this country's few Colonial-era mills that are still standing and, believe it or not, operational. Built in 1747, The Mill at Anselma was a working mill until well into the later part of the 1900s. By 1982, when the French Creeks Conservation Trust purchased the mill, it was no longer operating as a full-time business. Instead, the historic value of the property was of paramount significance, and the focus of those involved with the site shifted to one of preservation. Today, The Mill at Anselma Preservation and Educational Trust is charged with the responsibility of maintaining the property and sharing its value with visitors who tour the site. Tourists can take in the original workings of the grist mill along with its surrounding buildings, such as the Simmers-Collins and Miller's family homes, the Cider Press and the Creamery. In 2005, the mill was designated a National Historic Landmark.

Make a Note of It!

Most of us take it for granted and find it tough to make it out to the recycle center to do the ecologically friendly thing and have it recycled, but without it, we'd be in dire straights. Can you guess what am I talking about? That's right, paper. No, the computer has not—and will never—replace the need for paper, and here in the United States the production of paper began with a small mill near Philadelphia. William Rittenhouse established the Rittenhouse Mill in 1690. Born in Germany in 1644, Rittenhouse used the knowledge he gained as a papermaker in Holland to set up the historic mill. Floods destroyed the original building in 1701. The replacement building was destroyed by fire, and a third building survived until the late 1800s.

During the years the mill was in operation, a small community, known as Rittenhouse Town, sprang up around it. By 1890, the City of Philadelphia had purchased the mill and the original homestead. Over the years, more properties sold until most of the area known as Rittenhouse Town was owned by the city. For a short while, buildings were being demolished, including the mill, to make way for the development of Fairmount Park, one of the largest city parks in the country. A noble cause, to be sure, but in time, it was recognized that preserving our paper-making history was also important, and in 1984 the Friends of Historic Rittenhouse Town was formed.

Today, the entire area has been designated a National Historic Landmark District. Some of the original buildings that were not dismantled are being preserved. A barn papermaking studio is located on-site, and the history of papermaking in the U.S. is cata-logued and shared with anyone interested in learning more about it.

Mushrooming into Stardom

For a town with a population of 5273, according to the 2000 Census, Kennett has a lot to be proud of. Not only is it a commu-nity that prides itself on its varied history, it leads the country (some say the world) in mushroom production. Yup, folks in that neck of the woods call themselves the "Mushroom Capital of the World."

Road to Freedom

Although the practice of slavery isn't something that demon-strates America's greatest moments in history, there are parts of the story that offer a glimpse of what this country was really made of. The small community of Kennett is just one of many such examples. Visitors to the area would do well to take in the hour-long narrated tour of the Kennett Underground Railroad in the center's 20-passenger van and visit the town's more than 30 Underground Railroad sites. Aside from Thanksgiving and Christmas Day, the center is open for business and is eager to show the historic contribution early residents of the area made in helping a great many slaves in their quest for freedom.

STRANGE STRUCTURES AND BIG THINGS

Civil War Monument

Along with the historic buildings gracing the downtown core of Bloomsburg, visitors to the city won't be able to miss its Civil War Monument. Erected in 1908, the statue measures 60 feet in height and "commemorates eight Civil War campaigns in which Columbia County residents served and died."

Just for Mom

Want to do something special for mom this year? Take her to Ashland, where you can gaze on the Mother's Memorial together. True, this bronze statue, which is based on James McNeil Whistler's *Arrangement in Grey and Black* (better known as Whistler's Mother), isn't the cuddliest of moms. In fact, she's pretty grim. Commissioned in 1937 by the Ashland Boys Association, the eight-foot statue sits upon a piece of granite that is engraved with the following message: "A mother is the Holiest thing alive." Maybe, but would it hurt her to smile a bit?

Alcoa Building

This story isn't about a building that's overly large or oddly shaped so much as it is about a building constructed in a unique way. The Alcoa Building was opened in 1953 and was designed, according to the building's website, as "a showpiece of the use of aluminum in building construction." Aluminum replaced other more traditional building products in a number of areas—when it came to the outer "skin" of the building, for example. This made the entire structure lighter, and saved money in the process. It was one of the first buildings to use such large quantities of aluminum.

Larger than Life

Pennsylvania lays claim to several monuments larger than any other similar likeness in the world:

☛ Who doesn't know and appreciate that loveable bear named Yogi? His celebrity status is highlighted by what some sources call the "World's Largest Yogi Bear," located at the Cook Forest State Park.

☛ The "World's Largest Shoe" is not just fancy footwear. In fact, it can accommodate much more than a single sole. It's the Hallam Shoe House, located on the Lincoln Highway and recognized as one of the "World's Largest Things." Shaped like a workman's shoe, the one-of-a-kind house was built in 1949 by Colonel Mahlon Haines. It is built on five levels and measures 40 feet long and 28 feet tall. The giant shoe is made of wood, steel and wire, and it is covered with stucco 2 inches thick.

☛ What's touted as the "World's Largest Clothespin" is on dis-play at Philadelphia's City Hall. It's difficult to know what the motivation behind the building of this unique art piece was—the 45-foot, 10-ton steel clothespin sculpture is quite a contrast to the ornate, 19th century structure housing city hall.

☛ Many communities have a donut structure they believe to be the world's largest, and Pennsylvania is no different. The state's claim to large-donut fame is perched over a Maple Donuts outlet in Yokumtown.

☛ Thomasville is said to be home to the world's largest kettle, but when seen in photos, the kettle looks more like a soup pot—the kind you crisp potato chips in. According to one source, the kettle measures 6 feet tall and 4 feet wide, and it is made up of "mixed material."

☛ Holy mother of advertisements, Benjamin Moore & Co. sure know how to get the word out about their product—in particular their exterior soft gloss MoorGlo. The company has the "World's Largest Paint Can," which is near Shippensburg.

Tiny, Tiny Town

Although most folks seem to think bigger is better, the owners of Tiny World, near Shippensburg, think smaller is so much sweeter. Tiny World is really a miniature city with all the amenities populated by cats—yes, cats. There are gas stations, log cabins, a general store, town hall and church, a train station and assorted other buildings. Local folklore has it that strays from around the area have squatted there at one time or another. Ernest Helm built Tiny World in the late 1980s.

EERIE HAUNTINGS

Hex Murder House

This one's a definite must-see for anyone with a taste for the macabre. What is known as the Hex Murder House, located on Rehmeyer's Hollow Road in Shrewsbury, recounts the story behind the "Witch of Rehemeyer's Hollow." The story goes that a stretch of poor luck and some "other worldly" ideas tossed about between three witch doctors led to the homicidal behavior of the night of November 28, 1928. At exactly one minute past midnight, a Pennsylvania Dutch witch named John H. Blymire and his two accomplices murdered Nelson D. Rehmeyer (also known as the River Witch of Marietta). Blymire believed Rehmeyer had put a hex on him, and he claimed that the oppression he felt lifted as soon as the offending witch was murdered. The trio later burned Rehmeyer's body and scoured his home for a book entitled *Long Lost Friend*, a rare book published in 1846. They never managed to find the book, and the three men were captured and tried for murder, almost traumatizing the community, which apparently had no idea modern-day witchcraft was being practiced in their midst. Since Rehmeyer was murdered, the community has believed his house to be haunted, but it's never been demolished. In 2007, an entrepreneur transformed part of the house into a ghostly exhibit of sorts, and by October of that year, some public tours were conducted to select members of the public. It's still not a permanent attraction, but a little sweet talk to the owners of the house might get you a sneak peak—it's well worth the try.

GHOST TOWNS

Abandoned—Or Not?

Like any place with a history, Pennsylvania has its share of ghost towns. Every one of these communities, along with the many more that have been forgotten over the years, whisper memories of a time long since past...stories of the people who founded this great state.

☛ If you're driving along Route 61, you might not even recognize it when you pass a part of Pennsylvania history, but the community of Centralia was once a thriving coal-mining town. A fire in 1962 began burning in an abandoned coal mine outside town, eventually spreading to abandoned mines beneath the town. The government attempted to put out the fire but failed. Worried by the gases drifting out of cracks in the earth and the possibility of mine subsidence, residents began leaving Centralia in 1970. In 1981, when a cave-in in a resident's backyard resulted in a 12-year-old boy falling into a hole filled with carbon monoxide, the federal government began buying resident's property in an effort to relocate the town. However, a handful of stubborn folks still remain behind—and some visitors say the place is haunted. If you check out where the fire started, in an old mining pit, it's still burning to this day!

☛ The town is known simply as "#8," in reference to a mine in the area. According to one source there's little more than a few remains of company houses and bits and pieces of the mine.

☛ Remnants of the odd house foundation, an old cemetery circa the 1830s, and the hint that at one time there was something far more here is all you'll find when you pass by Gold Mine in Schuykill County. Apparently there was once gold (the black gold of anthracite coal, no doubt) in these hills!

☛ Morrison Town is located in Warren County. According to one report, there's not much to see in the area. A good deal of the region is underneath 130 feet of water, flooded out by the building of the Kinzua Dam. There are, however, two tombstones in the area. One mentions one of the founding family members, a Samuel Morrison. The other is a grave of a young boy named Samuel B. Stanton.

☛ What remains of Parker's Glenn (originally named Carr's Rock) are a few foundations, pipelines, railroad tracks and a water tower. The larger part of what was once a thriving community disappeared into the Delaware River after a hurricane in 1955. The town was once famous for its bluestone quarries—bluestone is a semi-precious dolerite used to make jewelry.

☛ If you ask folks in Venango County if there are any ghost towns in the area, there's a good chance they'll tell you about Pithole City. The community was the site of several oil strikes in the 1800s, and in 1865 Pithole City was founded. People flocked to the area, catching gold fever, and soon the population topped the 15,000 mark. Just as quickly, that number fell to 2000 and continued to dwindle until the community was nothing more than a tourist attraction. Since 1961, the Pennsylvania Historical and Museum Commission have managed the site, and visitors today can tour a visitor's center, a museum and a few scattered building remnants.

☛ Located in Sullivan and Wyoming counties, the community of Ricketts was once a thriving lumber community. The Trexler and Turrell Lumber Co. was founded there in 1890, and the company razed 5000 acres worth of virgin lumber. By 1913, the town had become a ghost town. Ironically, what sprang up around the area is Rickettes Glen State Park— a natural area and National Natural Landmark. The remains of what was once the lumbering community are located less than 5 miles north of the gate entrance.

CHECKING OUT THE FESTIVALS

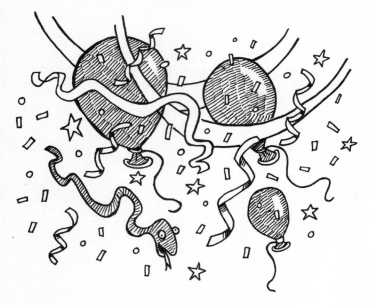

Bluegrass Bonanza

Newfoundland has been the site of the Pocono Mountains Bluegrass Festival since 1996, and it just keeps getting bigger and better every year. The event, hosted by the Blue Ridge Mountain Boys, runs for four days every June and offers a huge line-up of talent, along with ample opportunities for jamming—and it's not the only Pennsylvania festival to do so. The Appalachian Fiddle and Bluegrass Association has entertained crowds in Northampton County since October of 1973. Canyon Country Bluegrass Festival promises to warm the winter blues every February. The OATS Bluegrass Festival is held at the Benton Rodeo Grounds in July. And in February 2008, Wilmington joined the bluegrass bandwagon by hosting its first annual Wilmington Winter Bluegrass Festival.

Fun With Fungus

Did you know that when Kennett Square began cultivating mushrooms in 1896, it was the first place in the entire country to do so? Capitalizing on its status as the "Mushroom Capital of the World," Kennett Square has hosted a Mushroom Festival since 1986. The festival takes place over two days every September. Visitors, and there are usually about 110,000 of them every year, have a chance to buy mushrooms—and mushroom-related merchandise—tour the farms, eat mushrooms prepared in a variety of mouthwatering ways, as well as learn everything imaginable about the famed fungi.

All About Herbs

Since 1999, folks down in York have hosted the annual Pennsylvania Herb Festival. Educating people on the health and culinary attributes of different herbs is a huge focus of the conference, with a line-up of guest speakers discussing everything from Aromatherapy for Health and Wellness to Cooking with Herbs and Designing and Planting an Herb Garden. But it's not all work and no play. A wide assortment of vendors offers visitors a chance to check out herb-based products they might otherwise not have been aware of, and to take part in workshops, such as how to make specialty soaps and lotions. Herbs are often beautiful to look at, too, and each year one is chosen as the Herb of the Year. In 2008, the lucky candidate to fill that position is the yellow-flowered Calendula.

Medieval Mysteries

Back in the fall of 1988, a group of students, with a little prompting from professor Charles Scanzello, expressed a desire to learn more about all things medieval, and they formed the Kutztown University Medieval and Renaissance Club (KUMRC). Basically, the group is a campus-based branch of the Society for Creative Anachronism, and, as such, they get involved in recreating medieval life in every way, from feasts and fashion to swordplay. The group hosts the KUMRC Annual Renaissance Faire, sharing what they've learned about this way of life with curious visitors.

Celebrating the Harvest

Since 1964, Bedford has celebrated the fall harvest and the vivid, brilliant colors brought on by the change of seasons with its annual Fall Foliage Festival. Music is a big draw to this four-day event, as with most festivals, but where Bedford really shines is in the amazing array of craft vendors—more than 400, in fact. With everything from hand carved furniture and woven baskets to porcelain dolls and dried flower arrangements, there is no shortage of spending options. There's also a vintage car parade, a quilt show, food booths, children's activities—the list is endless.

Marching Along

The exciting thing about festivals in Pennsylvania is that there is such a variety of themes. Here are a few more options to check out:

☛ The Bach Festival in Bethlehem celebrates the oldest Bach Choir in the country. The choir was founded in 1898, and by 1907, it hosted its first festival. In case it hasn't hit you already, the festival celebrated its 100th anniversary in 2007.

☛ Bucks County celebrates its bounty with the annual Strawberry Festival, held the first weekend in May—but it's far from the only festival held in that area. Since 2004, the community has hosted an annual Celebration of Freedom in July; a Scarecrow Festival (which kicks off a lengthy scarecrow-making contest in Peddler's Village) and an Apple Festival in November; a Christmas Festival in December; and several others throughout the year. Folks living anywhere near Lahaska and Peddler's Village can't complain about a shortage of things to do!

☛ The Pennsylvania German Festival in Kutztown has welcomed visitors since 1950. As the name suggests, the German heritage is celebrated here with traditional crafts, music, food and more, mingled with all the good stuff life has to offer today.

☛ The Audubon Art and Craft Festival is hosted in Hawley every July. Nature is celebrated here with a wildlife art exhibit as well as nature films that run throughout the two-day event. Kids can take part in puppet shows, balloon sculptures and face painting, and live birds of prey are on site for all to see at the Delaware Valley Raptor Center.

☛ The 1000 acres of woodlands and meadows surrounding Hibernia County Park near Wagontown are alive with the sound of music for one day every August. For the last 80 years, literally hundreds of musicians have gathered in what's come to be known as "Fiddler's Field" for a day of joyful jamming!

TRUE ORIGINALS & PIONEERS

State of the Art Arena

The signature dome-shaped Mellon Arena, originally known as the Pittsburgh Civic Arena, took four-and-a-half years and $22 million to complete. It finally opened its doors on September 19, 1961. Nicknamed "the Igloo," this arena is the oldest of its kind still being used in the National Hockey League. However, its main claim to fame is that it's believed to be the first auditorium in the world to sport a retractable roof. Today, the arena is used primarily for sporting events, but it was originally built for the Civic Light Opera. The Opera had to find a new venue because the arena's acoustics were less than adequate for the job.

A Tragic First

Most of us wouldn't mind being first at something, but chances are the Ross family of Philadelphia would have gladly passed on the opportunity. On July 1, 1874, the family made headlines after their four-year-old son Charley was abducted from the front yard of their home in the Philadelphia suburb of

Germantown. Two men propositioned young Charley and his older brother, Walter, offering them a ride to a store to buy fireworks. While Walter entered the store to make his purchase, the men left with Charley. Shortly after the abduction, ransom demands were made to Charley's father who, in turn, went to the police. Although attempts were made to pay the kidnappers, a successful drop was never made. Charley was never seen again, but his sad story made history as the first kidnapping for ransom in America. Despite rumors that Charley was murdered, the family never gave up looking for their lost child.

Easing the Pain

They call it "the First House that Love Built," and it couldn't be a more apt description of the Philadelphia Ronald McDonald House. The story begins with Fred Hill, a Philadelphia Eagle football player, back in 1973. His three-year-old daughter Kim had just been diagnosed with leukemia, and Fred wanted to do something to make the treatment period easier to cope with for parents and patients alike during this horribly stressful time in their lives. When he spoke with his daughter's physician about what could be done in this regard, Dr. Audrey Evans expressed a need for a "home away from home" for patients who had to travel for treatment. From there, Hill's teammates joined forces with McDonald's Restaurant owners in Philadelphia, and their joint efforts resulted in enough money to purchase a home near the hospital. Renovations were completed in short order, and by 1974 the first-ever Ronald McDonald House opened its doors— organizers decided to name the house after Ronald McDonald only partly because of the support received from the franchise. Just like the restaurant, Ronald McDonald Charities has grown—almost 300 homes in 30 countries. The name was chosen "because of the positive, hopeful and fun-loving feeling this beloved clown inspires children."

Philadelphia Skating Club and Humane Society

Linking a skating club with the Humane Society wasn't such a stretch back in the days when the Philadelphia Skating Club and Humane Society was founded. The Skater's Club of the City and County of Philadelphia formed, on December 21, 1849. Members of this first skating club on the continent were basically folks who liked skating on frozen ponds and rivers. The sport could produce its own hazards, so club members took it upon themselves to wear identification badges and carry twine in case they should come across someone who'd fallen through the ice. The practice gave the club a bit of a humanitarian feel, so when the Humane Society of Philadelphia folded (that group started operating in 1770; its mandate was based on the Royal Humane Society of London and included all kinds of rescue work) it seemed a good fit to join the two groups. On February 28, 1861, The Skaters Club of Philadelphia became The Philadelphia Skating Club and Humane Society.

Preserving Nature's Beauty

If we allow ourselves to be observant, sometimes the simplest of nature's treasures jump out at us and stop us in our tracks. That's exactly what happened to a Quaker farmer named John Bartram. More than 250 years ago, the Bartram family farmed just 15 minutes from what is now the center of Philadelphia. While he was plowing his field one day he noticed a daisy, it's simple white petals bending slightly in the breeze, and he was entranced by its beauty. From that moment on, the Bartram family worked together to explore their natural surroundings, and to learn all there was to know about them and how to save them. They went on to form Bartram's Garden. The 45-acre site includes a number of gardens and natural wetlands, historic buildings, trails, unique trees and even an archaeological dig— one that's considered by some to be the "best preserved archaeological site on Philadelphia history in one location."

Separation of Church and Bridge

In 1926, the city of Philadelphia decided to build the Benjamin Franklin Bridge over the Delaware River to New Jersey. There was one little problem. On the Philly side of the river, right where they wanted to build the bridge, was a church. Not just any church but the St. George United Methodist Church that was founded in 1796. The small but spunky congregation headed to court and forced the bridge designers to move the bridge over 14 feet. Good idea. Today St. George's is not only known as "the church that moved a bridge"; it is also the oldest Methodist church in continuous use on the United States.

 With more than 200 covered bridges, Pennsylvania has the most in the nation. The first one was built over the Schuylkill River in the early 1800s by a Massachusetts carpenter named Timothy Palmer. The covered bridges are also called "kissing bridges" because a couple out for a buggy ride could take advantage of the bridge's privacy to sneak in a few smooches. A covered bridge spanning Roaring Creek in Knoebels Amusement Park celebrates bridge romance—hundreds of couples have carved their initials in the bridge's posts.

First for the Governors

Pennsylvania has had 51 governors since Thomas Wharton Jr. was appointed governor in 1776. Technically, he was called President of Pennsylvania (had a nice ring, didn't it?) but the job was the same as governor. By 1790, President of Pennsylvania was out and Governor was in. Governor Thomas Mifflin to be exact. It wasn't until 1911 that a foreign-born gent took the reins. That man was John Kinley Tener. Born in Ireland in 1863, he held the governor's position from 1911 to 1915.

A First For Women

America's National Woman Suffrage Association made history on July 4, 1876, when the group produced the "Declaration of Rights of the Women of the United States" and presented the document during a centennial celebration at Philadelphia's Independence Hall. With five simple but strong and indisputable statements, the authors of this document set the foundation for equality and personal rights for women. Susan B. Anthony read the document to those who had gathered. It was later framed and now hangs at the Capitol building in Washington, D.C.

Setting the Stage

When it comes to setting a precedent, the City of York considers itself front and center—both in the state and in the country. Although residents of York claim that theirs was the first capital city of the United States, quite a few other cities claim the title of capital for themselves—including three Pennsylvania cities.

Philadelphia (1774–77)—Men from the original colonies met in the city to lead the new nation—or rebel colony, depending on who you asked. In Philadelphia, they wrote and approved the Declaration of Independence, our break with England, which allowed us to form a new country.

Lancaster (September 1777)—With Philadelphia in danger of a British invasion, the leaders of the Continental Congress abandoned the city. They moved briefly to Lancaster (for one day!) before settling for a lengthier stay in York.

York (1777–78)—After Lancaster, the Continental Congress headed for York, where the Articles of Confederation—our first government—was completed in November 1777.

Philadelphia (June 1778–83)—Once the threat of a British invasion had passed, the representatives returned the capital to Philadelphia, where they ratified the Articles of Confederation.

Philadelphia (1790–1800)—Princeton, Annapolis and Trenton each served briefly as the capital before the new government settled in New York City in September 1788. New York City became the capital under the Constitution in September 1788. After taking the oath of office in New York City, Washington quickly approved returning the capital to Philadelphia for the decade it would take to build the permanent capital.

When All Was Said and Done…

Washington DC—In 1790, President George Washington signed The Residence Act, which stated that the permanent site of the capital would be "directed on the River Potomac, at some place between the mouths of the Eastern branch and Connogochegue" as of "the first Monday in December in the year one thousand eight hundred." It may not have had a name—or even an exact location—but it ended up being Washington DC.

Its claim as first capital may be up for debate, but York has plenty of other firsts to its credit, according to its official website:

☞ The Articles of Confederation were completed in York.

☞ The words "The United States of America" were first uttered in this city.

☞ Yorkers consider their city the "home of the first Thanksgiving proclamation" in the country.

☞ The first church was a log building erected in York in 1744.

☞ Martin and John Schultz were the first settlers to build their home from stone. John's house was erected near Stony Brook in 1734, and Martin's house was built that same year in Hellam.

☞ The first road in York County was named Monocacy Road and connected Wrightsville to Virginia, following an old Indian trail. It was built in 1739.

☞ The first "iron locomotive" was made in York, as was the first steamboat.

☞ The first "place of public entertainment" in what is now the City of York was a hall built by Peter Wilt in 1812.

☛ The City of York is home to a number of amazing discoveries, not the least of which was the discovery of oxygen—in a clinical context, of course. The story goes that one Dr. George Holtzapple was anxious to help his young pneumonia patient breathe better. He collected "oxygen, chlorate of potash and black oxide of manganese," as well as an assortment of equipment and rigged a way to heat up the chemicals and direct the pure oxygen into the young boy's face.

☛ As for famous scientific firsts, York was also home to Frederick Melsheimer and his sons, John and Ernst. The trio accumulated, catalogued and stored a huge collection of insect species from around the world, about 15,000 in fact, and in 1806 Frederick published *A Catalog of Insects of Pennsylvania,* the first study of its kind in the U.S. The work contributed to the Melsheimer men being heralded as the "fathers of entomology in the United States." The Melsheimer Collection is currently housed in Harvard College.

DID YOU  KNOW?

Although he selected the site, visited several times during construction and even allowed the naming committee to bestow his family name on the permanent capital of the United States, George Washington never lived in Washington DC. During his Presidency, he lived in Philadelphia and, after refusing a third term in 1797, retired to Mount Vernon, Virginia. The city on the Potomac didn't officially become the capital until 1800, one year after Washington's death.

Advertising Opportunities

Pennsylvania decided to show the world it was "high tech, high energy and ready for the new millennium" when, in 2000, it issued license plates with its state's website—www.STATE.PA.US.

Essentially, the license plates are like thousands of mini, roaming billboards. No longer would anyone have an excuse for not knowing where to get state information. In 2005, the license plate was revised again; this time the website visitPA.com replaced the first website. Now anyone sitting in traffic was reminded of the state's tourism website—a great way to promote your state, don't you think?

In 2005, Pennsylvania also became the first state to use blogs as a direct-to-consumer marketing tool. The state sponsored six different trips around the state, and in return, the tourists provided the state tourism site with blogs, digital photos and video of their adventures. The themes of the trips were culture, history, thrills for families, outdoor adventures, motorcyclists and couples. No boring brochures for PA.

Broadcasting Live!

Living in the 21st century, it's easy to take technology for granted. If we so choose, we can collect information from anywhere around the world easier than taking a trip to our local library. But in the early part of the 20th century, that wasn't the case. So when WLS Radio journalist Herb Morrison told his listeners about the Hindenburg airship bursting into flames over Lakehurst Air Station in New Jersey on May 6, 1937, it wasn't just the terror of the situation and the tragedy of 36 dead that made the news, it was the broadcast itself. The Chicago station was the first to broadcast coast-to-coast, and Pennsylvania-born Morrison was the man to do the job.

In Search of Uncle Sam

Choosing our nation's next president is always big news, and the first time live reports were televised from a presidential convention was in June of 1948. The venue was the Republican National Convention, held in Philadelphia, and the big news of the day was the nomination of candidate Thomas Dewey.

Sweet Silver Bells

George Schulmerich founded Schulmerich Bells in Sellersville in 1935. At the time, the company focused on building carillons, the stationary set of bells typically hung from a church tower and played by a keyboard. Schulmerich Bells is one of the largest producers of the product in the world, and in 1962 the company expanded its world-renowned reputation by introducing the production of English hand bells. It was the first company to manufacture the unique instrument in all of North America, and today the company calls itself "oldest existing hand bell manufacturer in the United States."

Parachuting into History

Stefan Banic, born in Nestich, Slovakia, in 1870, immigrated to the United States and settled down in Greenville in 1907. Initially, Banic worked as a coal miner and stonemason, but he was bright and had no end of ideas to tweak a tool or make a process more effective. He attended technical school at night and eventually funneled that inquisitive and innovative personality of his into creating new devices to make life better. His first remarkable invention was the parachute. He came up with the idea after witnessing a terrible accident. On June 3, 1914, he tested his creation himself by leaping from a 41-story building in Washington, D.C. He was granted the first-ever patent for a parachute on August 25, 1914, which he immediately donated to the Army Signal Corps and the American Society for the Promotion of Aviation. His invention didn't make him rich, nor did it gain him much recognition until after his death, but it accomplished something far greater—it saved lives. For Banic, that knowledge was very likely the best payment he could receive.

Sugary Sweet

Talk about patriotic. Back in the mid-1700s, new settlers to the Nazareth area were so taken by their new home they wanted to do something special to commemorate it. That's how the Nazareth Sugar Cookie was born. Made with a simple combination of flour, sugar, eggs, baking soda, vinegar, salt, milk and vanilla, what really sets this cookie apart from other sugar cookies is the fact that these newcomers to the western world perfected it, and they often baked it in the shape of a keystone. Since 1996, there's been an ongoing debate in the House and Senate whether to adopt the chocolate chip cookie or the beloved sugar cookie as the official state cookie. As of this writing, the dispute has yet to be resolved.

A Man of Many Firsts

David Rittenhouse was the kind of fellow who just focused his efforts on the task at hand—getting the job done was his main concern. Inevitably, folks with this kind of ability to concentrate become famous for one thing or another, their efforts usually paying off in some amazing way, and Rittenhouse was just such a fellow. He was born in 1732 and, though largely self-taught, worked successfully as an astronomer, inventor and mathematician. In those capacities, Rittenhouse was credited with a number of milestone accomplishments: he was one of the first people in the country to build a telescope; he created the first diffraction grating using hairs instead of wire; he discovered Venus' atmosphere in 1768; he was one of the founders of Philadelphia's Democratic-Republican Societies in 1793; from 1792 to 1795 he served as the first director of the United States Mint; and he and surveyor Andrew Ellicott were responsible for completing the survey of the Mason–Dixon line.

Beware!

The skull and crossbones image that typically appears on the containers of dangerous chemicals to warn users of the contents is a clear sign to most adults that the substance is poisonous. But after a study was conducted that asked children if they knew what the symbol meant, it was clear most youngsters didn't get the message. (In some cases children may have misinterpreted the image, linking the skull and crossbones to stories of pirates and thinking that drinking the substance was a good thing.) So in 1971, the Poison Center at Pittsburgh's Children's Hospital hosted a competition asking grade school students to come up with a design that kids would understand meant something was dangerous. Wendy Brown's image of Mr. Yuk won out over all other entries. Since then, the symbol of a sour-looking face is front and center in circular stickers, bordered by phrases like "Mr. Yuk means no!" or "Poison here."

INTERESTING HISTORY

Native Americans

In 1758, the Delaware (or Lenni Lenape) and Iroquois tribes who called Pennsylvania home gathered in Easton to try and secure a homeland within the state—the Wyoming Valley on the northern Susquehanna River. Their leader was Teedyuscung, who called himself "King of the Delawares." They were denied a place not only by the white settlers but also by members of the Iroquois tribe from New York, who claimed the land was theirs. Although a few members remained behind, trying to become more "white" by wearing European clothes and adopting European ways of life, most of the Lenni Lenape and Iroquois followed earlier Native American tribes who moved to the western section of the colony and eventually west of the Mississippi River. By 1800, there was only one small Seneca community, a member of the Iroquois Confederation, left in the entire state.

DID YOU  KNOW?

The first non-reservation school in the country for Native American children was established in Pennsylvania in 1879 at an abandoned military barracks. The founder, Richard Henry Pratt, was determined to assimilate the children from Plains tribes into the "white world," and he believed that, in western Pennsylvania, they would be isolated from any Native American influences.

In the Beginning...

In the beginning, the land that would become Pennsylvania changed hands more frequently than chips on poker night. First, the Swedes came into what would become Philadelphia County and established New Gottenberg and Tinicum (near the modern town of Chester) under Governor Johan Printz. For the next 20 years, they argued with nearby Dutch and English settlements. In 1655, Governor Peter Stuyvesant of New Amsterdam (modern New York City) took the land in the name of the Dutch government. The English Navy launched a surprise attack and seized Stuyvesant's land in the name of King James II's brother, the Duke of York, in 1664. (Two questions: Why not in the name of the King? And was the king insulted?) A decade later, most of what land was retaken by the Dutch. But it was the English who claimed what land they had managed to hold on to for their country and created Pennsylvania in 1681. Of course, who cares who claimed what and when? Eventually, they all lost it to those revolutionaries who started their own country—the United States of America.

DID YOU KNOW?

Governor Peter Suyvesant had a wooden leg—he lost his limb in a military battle against the Portuguese.

William Penn

You would think a guy who started a state would be your basic Type-A super-achiever, wouldn't you? Well, as far as William Penn's family was concerned, he was nothing to write home about. First, he got expelled from Oxford for being a little too puritan for the frat boys. Apparently they like their students wild and crazy. Although his family adhered to the official religion, Anglicanism, Penn had been interested in other faiths since childhood. When he was sent to Ireland on family business, he attended Quaker meetings and wrote a tract about his new beliefs. His writings landed the newest member of the Society of Friends (aka Quakers) in jail—one of several times Penn would be jailed for his religious beliefs. In 1681, King Charles II granted Penn a charter for a territory in the New World, in memory of Penn's late father, the admiral Sir William Penn. For the King, it was both a way to cancel a debt of £16,000 the elder Penn had loaned him and encourage religious non-conformists to leave England.

Because his religious beliefs were less than welcome in England, Penn decided that "Pennsilvania" [sic] or "Penn's Woods," named for his father, would be a "holy experiment" tolerant of all religions. He even signed a treaty with the local Native Americans and paid them for their land, two unusual events for the times, which resulted in a peaceful relationship between settlers and Native Americans for at least 70 years. On a personal note, Penn didn't do as well. Back in England, he landed in prison more than once—debtor's prison and for political reasons—before his death in 1718. In all, Penn only lived in the Commonwealth of Pennsylvania for about four years.

The First Civil War

In 1768, the Susquehanna Company made plans to settle an area given to Connecticut by King Charles II about a century earlier. When the Connecticut settlers arrived in the Wyoming Valley, they found an unexpected surprise—Pennsylvanians. Seems Charles, never a great guy with a map, had given the same land to both colonies at different times. Connecticut got their charter first, but Pennsylvania built their houses first. The two sides could have settled it by flipping a coin but decided that a war would be a much more effective decision maker. Let the Pennamite-Yankee War begin!

After the 1775 Battle of Nanticoke, the Connecticut fellows were declared the winners, but they allowed the Pennamites to stay. After the Revolutionary War, it looked like things would be heating up again (didn't fighting the British and Hessians tire these guys out at all?). Instead, Congress sent them to court where the dispute was decided in favor of PA. Once again the losing settlers were allowed to stay—though the Pennamites pushed them to the western section of the valley. So when you visit Wilkes-Barre, Nanticoke, Kingston and neighboring towns ask yourself: Are they Pennsylvanians or Connecticut Yankees masquerading as Keystoners?

First, There Was Pennsylvania

You can't talk about the creation of the United States without mentioning Pennsylvania...a lot! So let's narrow it down to the five top "Revolutionary" things that happened in PA during the birth of a new nation:

1. Instead of celebrating on Christmas night 1776, General Washington loaded his men in leaky boats and paddled across the Delaware River to New Jersey, where he attacked the Hessian soldiers hired by the English. It was the ultimate sucker punch because most of the Germans were drunk from a little too much celebrating. Although it's now

known as Washington Crossing (surprise, surprise!) in earlier years the town was known as Bakers Ferry, McKonkeys Ferry and Taylorsville.

2. The Declaration of Independence was signed and read for the first time in Philadelphia—on July 8, 1776. The document was printed on July 4, published in newspapers on July 5 and read throughout the colonies on July 8. So our first July 4 celebration was actually on July 8.

3. George Washington and his Revolutionary soldiers spent the winter of 1777–78 at Valley Forge wrapping their shoeless feet in rags and dining on raw flour.

4. The United States Marine Corps was started in—you guessed it—a tavern. On Nov. 10, 1755, Congress passed a resolution to create a Marine Corps and Robert Mullan, owner of Tun Tavern, became the first Marine recruiter. And what better place to recruit Marines than from his very own Philadelphia tavern?

5. Pennsylvania was the state where plenty of documents that star in today's history books were written—the Declaration of Independence, the Articles of Confederation and the Constitution. Representatives of Pennsylvania were also some of the key shapers of these documents. John Dickinson, a Philadelphia lawyer, chaired the committee to write the Articles of Confederation. The state's representative at the Constitutional Convention, Gouverneur Morris served as chairman of the committee that wrote the Constitution and is often referred to as the author.

PHENOMENAL PENNSYLVANIA
If you're tired of the predictable Christmas turkey, gifts and carols, you can spend the day at the annual re-enactment of the Washington Crossing. Anyone can participate—as long as you have a" historically appropriate outfit, including appropriate footwear and a doctor's

certificate." But don't show up as George—the National Park Service chooses who gets to be the General.

What a Wife!

Valley Forge was no picnic but Mary Hays McCauley of Carlisle still followed her husband William, a gunner in the Pennsylvania Artillery, to his winter encampment. But she didn't become famous until June 1778, during the Battle of Monmouth. The soldiers called her Molly Pitcher because she carried water to tired, wounded soldiers on the battlefield. Then, when her husband was wounded, she took his place manning a heavy gun. General Washington made her a noncommissioned officer, and she was known as Sergeant Molly. She was even buried with a cannon stand by her gravesite.

 DID YOU KNOW?

Some men have their name go down in history. Others have their penmanship go down in history. Timothy Matlack, a Pennsylvania delegate to the Continental Congress wrote the final copy of the Declaration of Independence. Jacob Shallus, the Assistant Clerk to the Pennsylvania General Assembly, was paid $30 to hand write the Constitution that now hangs in the National Archives.

Sin Tax

If you thought the Whiskey Rebellion was about a few tee-totalers from the Keystone State pouring whiskey down the drain, you obviously don't know the people from Pennsylvania very well. Instead, it was a mini revolution by a few folks defending their right to make whiskey and not pay taxes. It all started when President Washington learned that peace treaties end wars, but bills go on forever. He was trying to balance the new country's checkbook when someone suggested a tax on "distilled spirits" to help pay off the bills from the revolution.

After a quick vote in the winter of 1791, both houses of Congress agreed. They might have had second thoughts if they had consulted with their countrymen—especially those out west. Farmers in the isolated western sections of the new country often got their grain to the marketplace by distilling it—far easier to transport a few jugs of whiskey than wagons full of grain. The protests became violent in Pennsylvania: people were tarred and feathered, a tax collector was shot and homes were burnt to the ground. In 1794, the President sent 12,950 militiamen to the state to settle the Whiskey Rebellion.

Why You Should Never Buy on Sale

How do battles start? Does each side line up, wait for the referee's countdown and throw themselves into the melee? Not exactly. During the Civil War, General Lee was planning to lead his Army north and attack General Meade and the Union forces. Incredibly, the match that lit the powder keg was a boot sale. A division of Rebs read in the "Gettysburg Compiler" that "fine calf boots" were on sale and—tired of their shabby footwear—decided to sneak into town and "buy" a few pairs of boots. Before they found the shoe store, they found Federal cavalry scouts, and KABOOM! The keg was lit.

The Battle of Gettysburg was a three-day battle fought in and around the town of Gettysburg that started on July 1, 1863. It was the farthest north the Rebels ever got, and it is considered

the deadliest battle for U.S. forces, with between 36,000 and 51,000 men killed in action. The two armies that battled were Lee's Army of Northern Virginia and Meade's Army of the Potomac. Almost one-third of the 97,000 Union soldiers were from Pennsylvania. Even though the war lasted for two more years, it was the beginning of the end for the Rebels. Not only their bodies, but also their spirits, were shattered by their loss in this battle.

President Abraham Lincoln traveled by train to Gettysburg in November to help dedicate the Soldier's Cemetery and made his most quotable speech—the Gettysburg Address. "Four Score and seven years ago..." That's 87 years, if you're wondering.

DID YOU KNOW?

In 1974, a privately owned 307-foot tower overlooking the Gettysburg battlefield was built for tourists. For years, a battle raged between historical preservationists and those who liked that the tower was the only place where you could see the entire battlefield. In 2000, the U.S. government took the owners to court, wanting to demolish the tower and restore the site to how it looked when the Civil War battle was fought in 1863. On July 3, the anniversary of Pickett's Charge, Controlled Demolition Inc. of Baltimore demolished the tower, free of charge.

Everybody Needs Money

Where do new governments get money? If you're the United States of America, you melt down some of your new president's silver and mint coins. The Mint in Philadelphia was the first federal building established and cast its first coin in 1793. The machinery that cast the first run—11,178 copper coins—was run by horses. And who guarded all that money? A dog the government bought for $3.

PENNSYLVANIA DUTCH

The most well-known community in the state isn't north, south, east or west. In fact, it isn't a place at all. Instead, it's a cultural community—the Pennsylvania Dutch. Seems pretty straight-forward, doesn't it? Pennsylvania Dutch...Dutch people who live in Pennsylvania, right? You would think so, but that isn't the case at all. In fact, the origins of the Pennsylvania Dutch are the result of a shtick worthy of Abbott and Costello.

Time: Pennsylvania countryside pre-1800
Setting: Fence that separates two farms

English Farmer: Hey, you're new. What are ya? Swede?
German Farmer: Deutsch.
English Farmer: Dutch?
German Farmer: No, no. Deutsch.
English Farmer: That's what I said, Dutch.
German Farmer: NO. Deutsch!

English Farmer returns to his farmhouse in disgust, where his
  wife is waiting.

Wife: Are the new neighbors nice?
English Farmer: They're a bunch of dumb Dutchmen.

Repeat this scene hundreds of times with German immigrants
all over the state and a new group is born—the Pennsylvania
Dutch (also known as the dumb Dutchmen). Except they
weren't Dutch. Or dumb. They were German—*Deutsch* in their
native tongue—which they patiently told their neighbors over
and over again. Being christened Dutch wasn't the only misun-
derstanding these new immigrants had where language was concerned. What's come to be called the Pennsylvania Dutch
language is actually a German dialect called *Pfalzisch*, familiar
to those still living in a south-western section of Germany.

What's That You Said?
Combining Pennsylvania Dutch with the English the settlers
learned often resulted in some unusual twists. Sometimes
thoughts translated from German to English came out a little...
unusual.

The potatoes is all. (The potatoes are all gone.)

The stuffing is yet. (There is still some stuffing left.)

John et himself already. (John finished his meal.)

I must change around. (I must change my clothes.)

How long is your off? (How long is your vacation?)

What fer book? (How much do you charge for the book?)

I'll drop up this evening. (I'll come for a visit this evening.)

It's making down hard. (It's raining [or snowing] hard.)

Throw the horse over the fence some hay. (Throw some hay over the fence to the horse.)

Just make on when they ask. (Pretend you know the answer when they ask.)

You're a good piece off. (You're far from home.)

A Shared Tongue

But their neighbors quickly became accustomed to the language oddities and even adopted a few of the German words that the Pennsylvania Dutch sprinkled into their conversations.

Blabbermaul—talkative (became blabber mouth)

Booghered Up—mixed up

Dummkup—idiot

Dunk—dip (donuts in coffee)

Jonijumbubs—pansies (became Johnny Jump Ups)

Rootsh—wiggle or squirm

Spritz—spray

Wutz—piggie

They're Not all Amish

Although the most famous (they would cringe at that word) of the Pennsylvania Dutch are the Amish, who live mainly in Lancaster County, the group is much larger. First, there are the Fancy or Gay Dutch (if you are thinking what I think you are thinking—no, that's not what the name refers to). The Fancy Dutch are those who are Catholic, Lutheran, Reformed or other religions that don't require their people to practice "the old ways." They are assimilated into everyday life: they wear bikinis, listen to mp3 players and race cars (sometimes all at the same time). The only things that separate them from you and me are a few "Dutchie" words or sayings they may still use and some cultural foods they may enjoy.

The other group is the Plain People, which includes several religions: Amish, Moravian, Mennonite and others. Just as each group has different religious practices, so to do they have different ways in which they live their lives. Some blend into society well, seeming to be just a bit more modest than your average person, whereas others are obviously separate from modern society. The most traditional order is the Amish. Because they try to keep themselves separate from the modern world, many people have developed false ideas about their way of life.

Myth: The Amish believe taking their photograph will steal their soul.

Fact: The Amish aren't worried your little magic box is going to suck out their soul—but they are worried about vanity. They take the Bible verse warning against creating "graven images" very seriously. They don't want any photos taken with visible faces, including their children. They don't mind photos of their possessions or perhaps a long-distance shot of them in the buggy, but nothing that might tempt them to say, "Look at that pretty photo of me."

Myth: The Amish religion forbids them to use electricity, telephones or cars.

Fact: The Amish do not own cars or hook their homes up to the electrical power grid. Normally, they use a horse and buggy but will ride in a friend's car or hire a car (they'll also buy a train or plane ticket, if needed). They also light and heat their houses using generators powered by gas. Although they don't have phones in their homes, sometimes a phone will be located in a small outer building that several families share for business purposes or emergencies.

Myth: The Amish only wear black.

Fact: The Amish men do wear dark colored suits, suspenders, shoes, socks and hats, and the women wear black aprons, capes and coats. However, both men and women seem to make up for their required clothing by choosing especially bright colors for their shirts and dresses—bright blue, purple, even lime green. Females also wear a white or black prayer cap over their long hair. The Amish only wear certain types of clothing as a reminder that they want to remain separated from the world and to prevent vanity.

Myth: The Amish refuse to pay taxes.

Fact: The Amish pay all the taxes you and I do with one exception—they don't pay Social Security taxes if they are self-employed. And the IRS approves. It only seems fair because the Amish very rarely collect Social Security benefits, Medicare or Medicaid. They prefer to provide for their own people without government aid.

Myth: Amish religious beliefs forbid the use of doctors or hospitals.

Fact: Nothing in the Amish religion prohibits professional medical assistance. They will use both doctors and hospitals. Because they don't usually have medical insurance (some work for non-Amish employers where they receive medical benefits) the community joins together to help pay any medical bills that result from treatment.

Myth: The Amish dislike English people.

Fact: The Amish try to be understanding of all people and are often quite friendly and generous with their non-Amish neighbors. If you overhear them speaking disapprovingly about "English ways," they aren't just talking about tea and crumpets. The word "English" is used to describe anyone or anything that is non-Amish.

Myth: All Amish are farmers.

Fact: Many Amish are farmers, but others are artisans or tradesmen. Some also work for businesses owned by non-Amish.

A TOWN BY ANY OTHER NAME...

Phil Town Has a Nice Ring, Doesn't It?

Many towns are famous because a notable person calls the place home. Only one is famous because a notable groundhog calls the place home. Yes, groundhog. Punxsutawney Phil, Seer of Seers, Sage of Sages, Prognosticator of Prognosticators and Weather Prophet Extraordinary—known as Phil to his friends—calls the western Pennsylvania town of Punxsutawney home. Specifically, a climate controlled home within the local library, where he resides with his lovable wife Phyllis. Now Phil, being a literary type of groundhog, spends most of his days lounging around in the library, reading a few good books. He also enjoys a good movie, with his favorite being *Groundhog Day,* starring Bill Murray. Despite some Entertainment Channel rumors, he didn't turn down the opportunity to co-star opposite Murray in the movie. Phil's never been the Hollywood type.

February 2 is Phil's day to shine. Along with 30,000 of his closest friends, Phil treks up to Gobbler's Knob where, at 7:25 AM, he predicts whether or not we'll be having an early spring. Some people have been rude enough to suggest that, with all the camera flashes and television lights, neither Phil nor anyone else can tell if his shadow is showing. Ha! Phil can also rely on his super weather senses and just whisper his prediction in the ear of one of the Inner Circle. The Inner Circle is a group of Punxsutawney residents dressed in dark morning coats and top hats who accompany him on his annual weather forecast. His bodyguards, if you will. After all, somebody has to protect him from his enthusiastic and adoring fans.

Is Phil accurate? Of course! He's been doing this since the 1800s—"Punxsutawney Spirit," the local newspaper, first recorded his prediction in 1886. Of course, it all began long before that. In Europe, people relied on badgers or hedgehogs to predict whether there would be six more weeks of winter each Candlemas (February 2). When they immigrated to the United States and found the traditional predictors in short supply, people recruited groundhogs as stand-ins for their European counterparts. Other groundhogs may have tried, but only Phil has shown a special gift for weather predicting.

Naturally, Phil is an especially long-lived groundhog and will be celebrating his 125th birthday soon. Although he isn't very talkative during interviews, he's appeared on the *Oprah Winfrey Show* and he met President Ronald Reagan in 1986 (he loved the Rose Garden but was disappointed that he didn't get to sleep in the Lincoln Bedroom), and Pennsylvania governors Dick Thornburg and Ed Rendell. His only regret is that Punxsutawney, which means "town of the sandflies," was never renamed Phil Town. He still occasionally brings it up at town council meetings.

DID YOU KNOW?

Phil and Phyllis aren't the only groundhogs in town. There are 32 6-foot-tall fiberglass Phantastic Phils all around town. Sponsored by local businesses or organizations, the Phils started off exactly alike. Then each group personalized their Phil. Now he can be spotted around town delivering pizza, hauling luggage as a doorman at a local hotel, even doing his Statue of Liberty imitation.

A Cow With Wanderlust

Once upon a time there was an old woman who had a cow named Bola. Unfortunately, Bola was a great believer in the old saying "the grass is always greener on the other side of the fence." Because of that, the old woman spent a lot of her time searching for her runaway bovine. Daily, she could be seen (and heard) wandering through the streets of her small patch (coal mining town) like a town crier calling "Come, Bola! Come, Bola!" Now, to the immigrants pouring into town to work in the coal mines, this old woman was a mystery. It didn't help that they knew only a handful of English words. But in Polish, Lithuanian and Slovak, they talked to each other about this strange woman. When they visited other villages to shop, visit or attend church, new friends asked them where they lived. "Come Bola," they would answer with a smile, and everyone would know exactly which tiny patch they meant.

And that is how the town that some unimaginative person dubbed Hubbleyville became Cumbola. Some point out that *cwm bola* means "the valley belly" in Wales, a country that also supplied a large number of immigrant miners to the area. They then suggest that must be the origin of the name for this town of 400 that lies in a section of Schuylkill County called "The Valley." No, insist old-timers. It was the cow.

Where Can I Get a Shot and a Beer?

Many town names honor their founding fathers (Pottstown, Harrisburg), some describe the town (Hidden Valley, Little Meadows) and others are reminders of the old country (New Britain, North Wales). As a state founded to welcome those searching for religious freedom, Pennsylvania boasts plenty of towns with religious themes. Along with more than a dozen towns that start with Saint, the state also has Bethlehem, Nazareth, Emmaus, Damascus, Egypt, Calvin, Quakertown and Puritan.

Other town names have a less-than-heavenly inspiration. Often, the first public building to go up in a new town was the tavern (sometimes even before the houses). Every tavern has to have a name and, though they may not have known the name the founding fathers chose for the town, everyone knew the name of the tavern. Even if the townspeople couldn't read or didn't visit the tavern, it usually featured a painting hanging out front that represented its name. When asked where they came from, people would name the tavern and, before long, the official town name was forgotten. Some towns that can thank a tavern for their name are Red Lion, Lionville, King of Prussia, White Horse, Temple, Bull's Head, Cross Keys, Broad Axe and Blue Bell. The most famous "tavern town" is probably Bird-in-the-Hand. The tavern owner wasn't trying to shock people, just tell them he didn't take credit—only cash. Hence the painting of a songbird resting on a palm to represent the proverb "A bird in the hand is worth two in the bush."

Bird-in-the-Hand and Intercourse aren't the only towns that have visitors doing a double take. Pennsylvania also boasts Blue Ball, Climax, Paradise, Beaver, Manns Choice, Pillow and Pleasant Mount.

PHENOMENAL PENNSYLVANIA Which Pennsylvania town claims to have the most frequently stolen road sign in America? Intercourse, of course. Dorm rooms all over the state proudly display the signs that are perennially stolen as college pranks. Some residents claim city workers don't even bother to replace the sign anymore because it disappears by the next morning.

Beach Life

If anyone tries to sell you a vacation house at the Jersey Shore—cheap—make sure you think twice before you hand over that down payment. It's going to be quite a haul to the beach every day. Jersey Beach is right in the middle of Pennsylvania, and the closest you'll get to strolling along a beach is the shore of the

Susquehanna River. Originally, Jersey Beach was named Waynesburg, but the folks living just across the river in Waynesboro yelled "Copycat!" So Jersey Shore it became, in honor of town founders Reuben and Jeremiah Manning's New Jersey roots. Reuben and Jeremiah, why didn't you just name it Manningburg? You can also relive memories of summers at the shore with visits to the state's Beach Haven and Beach Lake.

Governor Town

When a French visitor to a small town was shown the town's natural spring, he remarked "la belle fontaine" meaning "the pretty fountain." Nancy Harris, wife of one of the town's founders and daughter of the other, thought it would be a nice name for the village her family was planning. So the small village became known as Bellefonte, but it appears to have been misnamed. If the founders had a crystal ball, they would have named it Ville de Gouverneurs—Governors Town. The town that has a population of just 6400 has been home to seven governors. Three Republicans served as the state's governor: James Beaver (1886–91), Andrew Curtin (1861–67) and Daniel Hastings (1895–99). Two Democrats also filled the role: William Bigler (1852–55) and William Packer (1858–61). William Bigler and his older brother John were sworn in as governor the same year—John had moved away from Bellefonte and was elected in his new home, California. Robert Walker, a Democrat, was appointed governor of the Kansas Territory in April 1857 by the only Pennsylvania president, James Buchanan. He resigned in December over a disagreement about the slave issue in Kansas.

S-K...no...S-C-O-O...no...S-C-U

Since the Scripps National Spelling Bee first began in 1925, only six winners of the nation's biggest spelling bee have been from Pennsylvania. This is astounding because, thanks to the Native Americans that populated the state, many Pennsylvania names defy all spelling (and pronunciation) rules. If they started including place names kids from PA would be a shoe-in. Here are a few that would make it to the final round.

Communities	Waterways
Aliquippa	Conodoguinet Creek
Aquashicola	Kishacoquillas Creek
Catasaqua	Monongahela River
Charleroi	Muckinipates Creek
Connoquenessing	Ontelaunee Creek
Hokendauqua	Pouquessing Creek
Llewellyn	Schuylkill River
Nesquehoning	Susquehanna River
Osceola	Lake Wallenpaupack
Punxsutawney	Youghiogheny River
Uwchlan	

COMMUNITY CLAIMS TO FAME

The Most Famous Island in the State

Near the end of May in 1979, just about every person in the state received an unexpected offer to visit an out-of-state friend or family member. Was it "Invite a Pennsylvanian Home" week? No, it was "Pennsylvania Is Going to Explode" week. Obviously that didn't happen, but for a few days the entire world was waiting for the big KABOOM. It all began at 4AM on May 28 when a water pump shut down at the Three Mile Island Nuclear Generating Plant outside of Harrisburg. Seems like a small thing, but apparently nuclear power plants can quickly collapse, like a row of dominoes. The pump was responsible for circulating the water into a cooling system. Without the cooling system, things got hot—the turbine stopped, the nuclear reactor shut down, pressure built up, valves opened, back up systems malfunctioned, and suddenly the nuclear reactor was melting down. By 9AM, everybody in Pennsylvania was wondering if they would be glowing by nightfall. It didn't help the public mood that just two weeks earlier *The China Syndrome,* a movie about a nuclear reactor meltdown, was released. The movie included a fictional nuclear power expert explaining that a meltdown could make an area the size of Pennsylvania uninhabitable. Thankfully, life didn't imitate fiction. People living within 5 miles of the reactor were temporarily evacuated until the accident was categorized as "contained" and the reactor was shut down—permanently. Cleanup cost the government $975 million. No one was killed or injured, and the level of radiation released into the atmosphere was judged to be safe. But no one wanted to be the next Three Mile Island; of the 129 nuclear power plants being built at the time, fewer than half were completed. And chili lovers added a new category to their cook-offs—Three Mile Island Chili.

DID YOU KNOW?

Most school mascots are furry, goofy characters. But the Williamsport High School mascot is quite a charming fellow sporting a top hat, cane and white gloves. No, their mascot isn't Fred Astaire—it's the Millionaire. In the late 1800s, the city had the most millionaires per capita in the country. West Fourth Street in Williamsport, home to men who made their money in the lumber industry, was known as Millionaire's Row.

Otherwise Known As...

Oil Creek Valley—The Valley that Changed the World

Williamsport—Millionaire's Row, Birthplace of Little League Baseball

York County—Snack Food Capital of the World, Factory Tour Capital of the World

Hershey—Chocolatetown, USA, or The Sweetest Place on Earth

Reading—Outlet Capital of the World

Indiana—Christmas Tree Capital of the World

Bellefonte—Home of Governors

Chester County—Mushroom Capital of the World

Pittsburgh—Iron City or Smokey City

Scranton—Electric City

Philadelphia—City of Brotherly Love

Hanover—Pretzel Town, USA

Punxsutawney—Weather Capital of the World

Kane—Black Cherry Capital of the World

PENNSYLVANIA OUTDOORS

White-tailed Deer: Bambi or Godzilla?

Neighbors in other states are often horrified by the fact that Pennsylvanians would hunt cute little "Bambi." In fact, deer season is so popular that many schools schedule the first day of deer season as a school holiday. We sympathize with outsiders whose only interaction with deer is through animated cartoons, but even non-hunting Pennsylvanians are quick to point out that when a 200 pound white-tailed deer bounds across the road at night and ends up crushing your car like a tin can, "cute" is not a word that comes to mind. When they aren't causing $130 million in car damage annually, these adorable animals are eating everything in sight to the tune of approximately $20 million in crop damage. Or giving birth—often to twins, sometimes even triplets. Unchecked, that could mean a lot of deer. Do we really want more deer in Pennsylvania than people?

Pennsylvania Water Adventures

Pennsylvania has more miles of river than any of the lower 48—more than 83,000 miles. Those rivers draw in plenty of Pennsylvanians to enjoy a watery adventure, ranging from a peaceful river sojourn in a canoe down the Clarion, Nashaminy or Delaware rivers to a wild white water rafting trip down the Lehigh and Youghiogheny rivers or Slippery Rock Creek. Kayakers flock to the Schuylkill, Susquehanna and Juanita rivers. In fact, Susquehanna University, only minutes from its namesake river, rents kayaks to its students so they can enjoy the river.

We also enjoy a bit of fishing. The lakes, streams and rivers of Pennsylvania offer everything from fly fishing or boat fishing to sitting on the bank and dropping in a line. Many towns sponsor

fishing rodeos for young fishers that offer prizes for the biggest (and littlest) fish caught—even though many of the young fishers choose to throw their catch back into the lake.

Grab Your Trail Mix

Pennsylvania also offers hikers a chance to attempt one of the ultimate hiking achievements—the Appalachian Trail. This 2175 mile trail travels through 14 states, from Maine to Georgia, and includes 232 Pennsylvania miles from the Delaware Water Gap to the eastern rim of Alleghenies then through the Cumberland Valley into Maryland. Hikers not up to the challenge of the Trail can try many of the other hiking trails that traverse the state.

LESS WHOLESOME ACTIVITIES

Do You Feel Lucky?

Pennsylvanians finally got tired of riding the bus to Atlantic City and legalized casino gambling in the state in 2006. Slot machines were legalized for 14 locations. Six are at already existing racetracks throughout the state, and others will be built in Philadelphia, Pittsburgh, Bensalem and Mt. Pocono. If you want to do a little betting but aren't interested in machines, you can visit Summerside Raceway, Pocono Downs, Philadelphia Park, Penn National Race Course or Ladbroke at the Meadows for harness and saddle races.

The most popular type of gambling in PA is the state lottery, established in 1971. Who can resist stopping at their local grocery store, take-out restaurant, gas station or newsstand on the way home from work for a quick pick? After all, for the bargain basement price of one measly dollar, you could win millions. And who hasn't played the "When I win the lottery..." game with their friends? Pennsylvania is the only state that uses its lottery profits solely to benefit older Pennsylvanians through such programs as a co-pay drug program, rent rebates and reduced public transportation fees. Since its creation, the lottery has contributed over $13 billion to programs for state seniors.

PA Party Time

After a 10-hour shift deep in a coal mine, tapping oil from the ground, cutting lumber or forging steel, you don't head down to the local bar and ask for a white wine spritzer. Pennsylvania is shot and beer country. Our blue collars may have whitened a bit, but our thirst for beer hasn't lessened. With 81 breweries, Pennsylvania ranks seventh in the nation. Most are microbreweries, with the largest being Yuengling Brewery of Pottsville, which produces over 500,000 barrels a year right in the heart of coal country. The brewery, which began in 1829 as the Eagle Brewery, is America's oldest. Founded by David G. Yuengling (ying-ling), it is still owned by the same family that began it—the fifth and sixth generations have taken over. The brewery even operated through Prohibition in the 1920s by making "near beer," which had only 0.5 percent alcohol. To celebrate the repeal of Prohibition in 1933, the brewery shipped a truckload of beer (renamed "Winner" beer just to remind everyone how that Prohibition experiment turned out) to President Franklin D. Roosevelt. No word if FDR enjoyed his gift from Coal Country.

Forget Eggnog—For a Real Christmas, You Need Boilo
For some people, the smells of Christmas are cinnamon, pine trees and baking cookies. These people have never experienced a Pennsylvania Christmas. If they had, they would know that the smells of Christmas are lemons, oranges, honey and cloves. These are the smells of boilo (boy-low) simmering on the stove. OK, technically the old-time Lithuanians will tell you that it's a drink they invented called *Krupnickas*. But "Krupnickas" was just a little too much for their Polish, Italian, Irish, German and Welsh neighbors to wrap their mouths around (especially after downing a few glasses of the stuff). So boilo it became. Now Emeril might call it a hot toddy with a little BAM. Don't make that mistake. In Pennsylvania, even little old ladies don't drink

hot toddies. However they do enjoy a little boilo. After all, it is medicinal—great for a chest cold or cough. Or could it be that after a sipping a few glasses you just forget you've got a cold?

Traditionally you start with some grain alcohol or moonshine (you don't think Southerners are the only ones with stills, do you?). Those of you that actually use your bathtub to bathe, just grab yourself some whiskey. Then stir in some orange and lemon slices, cloves, cinnamon sticks, allspice, honey, raisins and carraway seeds. Every family has its own secret recipe that is guarded and only handed down when the present boilo maker is on his or her deathbed. Only in Pennsylvania will families go to court over who gets grandma's boilo recipe.

DID YOU  **KNOW?**

Pennsylvania is the largest purchaser of booze in the world. No, it's not that our state employees are throwing a huge cocktail party every Friday. It's because Pennsylvania is one of the few states where you can only purchase wine and liquor at "state

CHUG
CHUG
CHUG

stores," retailers run by the state. Beer, on the other hand, is purchased at beer distributors. Neither can be purchased in grocery stores or convenience stores, though several state stores have been established within grocery stores in recent years (similar to a bank, sub shop or photographer putting one of their chain stores in the same building as a super-store). Weird huh? And very confusing to out-of-state visitors. Don't forget to plan ahead so you don't end up with a dry celebration on Memorial Day, July 4, Labor Day, Thanksgiving or Christmas. State employees—including those behind the counters at the state stores—don't work on state holidays.

"Ain't no party like a Scranton party—cuz a Scranton party don't stop."
–Steve Carrell (Michael Scott) of The Office

Drugs in Pennsylvania

Alcohol may be the drug of choice for most Pennsylvanians, but other drugs are not difficult to get. Most are moved through the state via Philadelphia or nearby New York City. The Drug Enforcement Agency lists marijuana, heroin, cocaine and crack cocaine and as the most readily available. Although meth and crystal meth users are concentrated mainly in urban areas, meth labs are increasingly being discovered in rural areas. It seems drug manufacturers are targeting rural counties because the smells and other signs of a meth lab aren't as easily noticed in these out of the way spots. In 2007, the DEA reported 813 drug violation arrests, up from 625 in 2003.

Outfest Comes to Philly

Because many Pennsylvanians have a strong tie to small towns and Christian religions, most of the gay-friendly spots are restricted to urban areas and non-religious college campuses. Pennsylvania's gay capital would have to be Philadelphia. In 2003, the city initiated a tourism campaign called "Get Your History Straight and Your Nightlife Gay." Philly is also a popular destination for two special events: Pride Day in June and Outfest in October. The first Outfest was celebrated in 1987, and with approximately 20,000 participants, it is billed as the largest celebration of National Coming Out Day in the world.

The Sexiest Spot in the State

The Poconos, a rustic mountainous spot in northeastern Pennsylvania, has had a few nicknames through the years. It started out as "Pennsylvania's Playground" in the 1920s— a name that evokes images of families vacationing in the woods while skiing, hiking, canoeing and enjoying the outdoors. During World War II, some called the area the "Friendly Mountain Resorts"—maybe this was because residents were always smiling, or it could have been because they turned a blind eye toward military personnel who brought their girl-friends to the Poconos for a final goodbye before shipping over-seas. Quite a few Lt. and Mrs. John Smiths checked in during the war years. After the war, those soldiers remembered the Poconos fondly and returned for their honeymoons (we can only hope with the same girl from that first visit). The Poconos became the "Honeymoon Capital of the World." Now it's the "Land of Love," thanks to Morris B. Wilkins, a resort founder. In 1963, Morris, a true romantic and creative guy, looked at one room's tub and said to himself, "Boring!" Before long, his Caesar Pocono Resort boasted the first heart-shaped whirlpool tub and was even featured in Life Magazine. A few years later, when Morris followed up his brainstorm with a 7-foot-tall whirl-pool shaped like a champagne glass, he was smart enough to patent the idea. So even though you may be able to find a heart-shaped whirlpool tub in 49 other states, there's only one state to go to when you long for a dip in a champagne glass. After the champagne tub, the Poconos jumped on the erotic bandwagon— you can find king sized round beds, mirrors (everywhere), glass enclosed showers, saunas for two, star-studded ceilings...think Las Vegas, but instead of showgirls and gambling they have trees and gambling.

HANGING AT THE HOSEY

The most remarkable chameleon in Pennsylvania would perhaps be the hosey. At the hosey, you can dance the Chicken Dance at your brother's wedding, hear a great rock band, get a delicious Sunday breakfast, win a ham or turkey (or occasionally even a lobster), take your mom to play Bingo or just hang out after work. Never heard of a hosey? For most people, it's also known as the hose company, fire station or FD. If your firefighters aren't so eager to have visitors, then you don't have a Pennsylvania fire department. In our state, the firefighters are our friends and neighbors. In 1736, Benjamin Franklin organized the first volunteer fire company in Philadelphia and, as far as volunteer fire companies are concerned, the state hasn't changed. Pennsylvania had the most volunteer fire companies in 1736 and still has the most today. When the last count was taken in 2005, the state had 2354 fire departments, with 2334 of those companies being 100 percent volunteer.

In most small towns throughout the state, when the fire whistle blows—day or night—men and women pour out of their houses and head for the hosey, jump on the trucks and roll away— ready to fight a fire, water down a highway after a car accident or search for a child lost in the woods. If the whistle blows again and again, people begin to worry. Either the incident is a really big one, or not enough fire fighters are answering the call. And we don't have a crew of professional firefighters waiting in the barracks of the fire company to rely on. If we don't fight it, who will? That's when the older "retired" volunteers head for the hosey to see if they're needed. In Pennsylvania, a volunteer firefighter never really retires.

When they aren't fighting fires or training to fight fires they are consumed with fundraising. Imagine how much gas it takes to

fill up a hose truck! These unpaid fighters—around 70,000 of them—risk their lives, educate the public about fire safety, and raise thousands of dollars each year. The money goes toward equipment upkeep and public programs. Halloween finds firefighters parked on roads with heavy traffic, escorting monsters and princesses across the street and handing out a few lollipops. They also make the rounds of elementary schools during Fire Prevention Week and high schools during prom season, doing their best to ensure they are never needed. So whenever true Pennsylvanians notice a firefighter standing in the middle of the road holding out a fire boot for the annual fundraising drive, they stop their car to toss in a few dollars. It's the cheapest fire insurance they'll ever get.

PHENOMENAL PENNSYLVANIA The nation's first female volunteer firefighter was Marina Betts of Pittsburgh, who joined in 1820. The 5' 2" member of the bucket brigade often got annoyed at male bystanders who didn't pitch in—Marina let her feelings be known by pouring a bucket of water over their heads.

MOVING INDUSTRIES

How Much Is In Your Wallet?

If you're from Pennsylvania, your wallet is about as thick as that of the average United States citizen. In 2005, the median household income for the state was $43,714 and for the country it was just a teensy bit more at $44,334. Although they did worse on unemployment (4.7 percent) than the country (4.6 percent), only 11.2 percent of Pennsylvanians were living below the poverty line compared with 12.7 percent of Americans.

The Gross State Product (GSP) of Pennsylvania is $468 billion, the sixth largest economy in the country and the 17th largest economy in the world. Pennsylvania's economy dwarfs those of such countries as Austria, Sweden, Switzerland and Egypt.

Imagine if There Was a Hurricane?

In 2008, *Overdrive Magazine* ranked Pennsylvania's Interstate 80, which runs from east to west, as the second worst in the nation. The only state with roads worse than ours is Louisiana— a state still struggling to recover from a devastating hurricane! Doesn't say much for the state's roads. Could it be because they're so old? In 1792, the nation's first macadamized toll road was the 62 miles that stretch from Philadelphia to Lancaster. Other major east-west routes are 76 and PA Route 6. If you're traveling north to south, try 79 or 81. But the majority of the roads are winding back roads that follow rivers and climb mountains while passing through tiny towns and farm fields.

All Aboard

Anyone who's counted Monopoly money realizes that Pennsylvania is a railroad state. Two of the game's railroads—Pennsylvania and Reading—are from our state. Pennsylvania's railroading history started in 1827 and became one of the biggest in the

nation, peaking at 11,551 miles of active track. In addition to using trains to haul anthracite coal and steel, Pennsylvania once built locomotives and rails. Even though industry and passengers don't use railroads as much anymore, train whistles still blow throughout the state. Train aficionados can also enjoy more than 20 tourist train excursions and visit Strasburg, home of the Railroad Museum of Pennsylvania; Scranton, home of the national park Steamtown; and Altoona's Horseshoe Curve, one of several amazing feats that make railroading possible in a state full of mountains, rivers and other engineering challenges.

DID YOU KNOW?

Almost 100 miles of old Pennsylvania railroad lines have been turned into 93 hiking, biking, snowmobiling and skiing trails throughout the state by the Rails to Trails Program.

Gondola, Anyone?

Venice, Italy, has turned its endless waterways and bridges into a romantic destination that attracts millions of visitors each year. Maybe somebody should tell Pittsburgh. Pittsburgh, a city where three rivers meet—the Ohio, the Allegheny and the Monongahela—is second only to Venice when it comes to bridges. Allegheny County has a whooping 1700 bridges with 720 of those within Pittsburgh city limits and 15 right in the heart of downtown. So why aren't honeymooners pouring in from all over the world to stroll the bridges hand in hand? Maybe it's because the only gondolas in town are special railroad cars used for shipping material such as timber, coal and steel.

Keystone Canals

In 1905, Thomas S. Allen wrote the song "Fifteen Miles on the Erie Canal" to commemorate the barges that were pulled from canal to canal by teams of mules (after the barges were converted to engine power). But he could have called it "Fifteen Miles on the Conwago, Beaver or Hudson Canal." There were a host of canals and locks in the state that joined the Delaware, Susquehanna and Schuylkill rivers and made it possible to deliver millions of tons of anthracite coal to New York and New Jersey until the turn of the century, when railroads took over the job.

CREATIONS OF THE COMMONWEALTH

Back-to-School Shopping

Crayola, once known as Binney and Smith, has been supplying school children with art supplies each September ever since the first eight-count box rolled off the assembly line in 1903. The Lehigh Valley company makes 5 million crayons a day—that's more than 2 billion a year.

America's Favorite Lighter

George Blaidsel was determined to invent a small, reliable lighter that could be lit with one hand. His laboratory was his Bradford garage, and he succeeded in 1932. Since the first Zippo lighters were manufactured in 1933, more than 425 million have been sold. During World War II, the normally shiny silver lighters were given a dull black finish and sold only to military personnel. Blaidsel was named "Mr. Zippo" by WWII correspondent Ernie Pyle. No matter how old your Zippo is, it has a lifetime guarantee—"It works or we fix it for free."

The First Family of Fireworks

When Antonio Zambelli came to New Castle from Italy in 1893, he brought his little black book with him. Mrs. Zambelli didn't have to worry—Antonio's little black book only contained formulas for fireworks. Thanks to that little black book, the third generation of the family is now making the fireworks seen at Times Square, Mount Rushmore and the Kentucky Derby.

Making Music

In 1839, C.F. Martin Sr., a German immigrant, moved his instrument making business to Nazareth. One million guitars and seven generations later, Martin guitars have made music with Eric Clapton, Gene Autrey, Sting, Jimmy Buffet, Johnny Cash and more. A Martin guitar even orbited the Earth with the crew of the Columbia Space Shuttle in 1994. Martin now sells more guitars than any other manufacturer in the nation—more than 90,000 a year.

INDUSTRY TODAY, GONE TOMORROW

Three of the industries that helped build not only Pennsylvania, but the entire country, are shadows of their former selves. But there was a time when the state's oil, coal and steel helped move the nation into the boom time that was the Industrial Era.

Black Gold

Prior to the 1800s, the world was lit up with whale oil. Although lanterns that used whale oil worked fine, there were two problems: the oil smelled (it was after all, burning whale blubber) and it was expensive (it cost quite a bit for Captain Ahab to go sailing around the world after whales). When the kerosene lamp was invented in 1857, the Canadians began drilling for oil and the Americans quickly followed—specifically, in Pennsylvania.

From Blacksmith to Oil Driller

For generations, the Seneca Indians of Pennsylvania had been gathering oil that seeped out of the ground and made its way to Oil Creek, where it lay on the surface. Whereas the Native Americans considered it medicinal, some Pennsylvanians processed it to use in lamps. The Pennsylvania Rock Oil Company, also known as the Seneca Oil Company, sent Edwin Drake to Titusville to search for oil. Colonel Edwin Drake was no oil expert; he was a former railroad employee who hadn't even seen crude oil. He must have prescribed to the "I'll know it when I see it" school of thought. When he managed to gather only about 6 to 10 gallons a day skimming the oil off Oil Creek, Drake decided that drilling was the only way to go. So who do you hire to drill for oil? A local blacksmith who drills wells, of course. Most local smithies thought Colonel was a bit "teched," but Billy Smith agreed to begin drilling in 1859. On August 27, just as Drake was considering giving up (he was just about out of money and the stockholders didn't want to contribute anymore) Smith hit 69.5 feet—and oil. It was the beginning of the state's oil boom.

Pennsylvania's Oil Boom

Soon everyone was heading to western Pennsylvania to sink their own oil well. Wells didn't produce indefinitely—a year was the average—but many oil drillers became millionaires. Initially the oil was transported by horse and buggy, but 1865 brought the first long distance oil pipeline in the country. The 5-mile pipeline led from Pithole to the railroad in Oil City. Teamsters (yes, there were even Teamsters back then), who had been growing rich hauling oil, were not thrilled with this new development. In fact, they attempted to rip up the new pipeline that was cutting into their bottom line. Sheriffs were put on pipe guarding duty. Eventually the Teamsters gave up. Between 1860 and 1870, approximately 17 million barrels of oil were shipped to the Pittsburgh area from Oil City. The oil industry lasted in Pennsylvania until the late 1920s and, until Texas tea was discovered in 1901, half of the world's oil came from Pennsylvania.

Colonel Edwin Drake was never in the military, let alone a colonel. His bosses thought the "colonel" might impress the locals. It didn't. They still thought he was nuts and called his scheme "Drake's Folly."

Black Diamonds

When you put together a cold hunter and a Pennsylvania mountain, what do you get? An industry that made the state billions of dollars. Rumor has it that in 1790, a hunter named Necho Allen was roaming the mountains of Schuylkill County in the eastern part of the state. Cold and tired at nightfall, he lit a campfire and dozed off. Imagine his surprise when he awoke to find the rocks surrounding his campsite on fire. Necho Allen had discovered that the veins of anthracite or "hard" coal that crisscrossed the northeastern part of the state could make an efficient substitute for wood in heating homes and fueling industries. It didn't take long for mines to spring up in the area and for tons of the shiny "black diamonds" to be shipped out of the area by barge and eventually rail. Around the same time, bituminous or soft coal was found in the western half of the state.

Working Underground

Mining is a dangerous job—since 1870 there have been more than 31,000 deaths in Pennsylvania's anthracite mines. This doesn't include the all-too-common nonfatal injuries—men have lost fingers and limbs or have been disabled in mine collapses. Because of this, most miners were new immigrants eager for any kind of work. Men from Germany, Wales, Poland, Ireland, Italy and Lithuania supported their families by working 12 hours a day in the darkness of the mines. They lived in company towns or "patches" within walking distance of the mines. These small patches became factories, supplying mine owners with a never-ending supply of cheap labor. Sons of miners were too poor to do anything but follow in their father's footsteps. Many boys starting working in the mines at age 8 as breaker boys and didn't stop until they died or were disabled. Often old men, not able to work underground anymore, returned to their first job— being a breaker boy picking rocks out of loads of coal. Meanwhile, mine owners were becoming millionaires.

Strikes, violence and lock-outs became common in the early 1900s when there were about 175,000 miners demanding better working conditions. The mining industry never recovered from the Great Depression, which brought both a decrease in demand for coal and the introduction of alternative fuel sources such as electricity, oil and natural gas. During World War II, coal was suddenly in demand again, and miners were exempt from the draft for their contribution to necessary war work. But after the war, demand for coal dropped, and most miners were out of work by the 1970s. The loss of jobs was only one facet of the problem when mines closed. Inactive mines usually filled up with water. Minerals leaching from the rock into the water make acid mine drainage the largest source of water pollution in the state—both by polluting waterways and becoming acid rain. Mine reclamation to help the environment has cost the state and federal governments more than 500 million dollars, and they expect to spend 15 billion more. Although the state is fourth in coal production, today there are only about 2000 miners, and mining contributes only about 1 percent of the Gross State Product.

DID YOU KNOW?

There are two types of coal in Pennsylvania—anthracite in the eastern part of the state and bituminous or "soft" coal in the western part. The state produces about 60 million tons of bituminous coal annually and 9 million tons of anthracite coal.

Building the Nation

When they tell you Pennsylvania built the country, they're usually talking in a dreamy way about the Declaration of Independence, the Constitution and breaking away from England (and they're right—we played a big role in that). But we also built it literally—the Brooklyn Bridge, the locks of the Panama Canal, the Chrysler Building, the Empire State Building, rails and locomotives, even the first Ferris wheel (designed by George Ferris, a Pennsylvania bridge builder). Without the iron and steel mills of western Pennsylvania, all those creations would have remained pipe dreams.

Steel: Winners and Losers

Depending your point of view, steel made us either the richest or the poorest people in America. Andrew Carnegie, from Pittsburgh, would vote for richest. When he sold his steel company to J.P. Morgan, he was crowned "the richest man in the world." Without a steel mill to keep him occupied, he turned to philanthropy—giving away $380 million to universities, museums, churches, libraries and other institutions.

Carnegie made a lot of money from steel—probably because his employees didn't. At the turn of the century, unskilled workers earned 15 or 16 cents an hour for a 12-hour day, and skilled workers could aspire to the grand sum of $6 a day. The private enforcers, the Coal and Iron Police, ensured that workers, police, towns, governments— just about everyone—did what was best for the mill owners. Even union organizers over- looked steel workers. They assumed the "Hunkies" (immigrants from southeastern European countries such as Italy, Poland, Russia, Greece, Serbia and Slovakia) were too dumb to organize.

They were wrong. When Franklin D. Roosevelt and his New Deal supported union organization and Governor Gifford Pinchot abolished the Coal and Iron Police, unions flourished. With the help of the United Steel Workers of America, steel work was a job that boosted blue-collar workers into the middle class after World War II. Then suddenly the steel industry collapsed in the 1980s, and more than half the jobs were lost. In mill towns like Allentown, Johnstown, Morewood, Dusquesne, Aliquippa, Bethlehem, Vandergrift and Pittsburgh, more than 200,000 people were out of work. Those jobs never returned, and the area became part of the "Rust Belt"—an area where the rusting machinery in silent factories and mills became a symbol for the decaying economy.

Billy Joel wrote a song about the downward economy in his hometown of Levittown, New York. But the name wasn't quite musical enough. Joel had played in Allentown—a town that was perfect for both the lyrics and the music. So it was "Allentown" that reached #17 on the Billboard Hot 100 and was included on five of his albums.

Well we're living here in Allentown
And they're closing all the factories down
Out in Bethlehem they're killing time...

Iron and coke
And chromium steel
And we're waiting here in Allentown
But they've taken all the coal from the ground
And the union people crawled away.

HEALTH

Long-lived

The average life expectancy in Pennsylvania is 76.7—number 31 on the list that has Hawaii at the top with 80 years and the District of Columbia at the tail end with a meager 72 years. Want to add a few years to your life? Move to Montgomery, Northampton or Union counties, all of which boast a life expectancy of 78.8 years. You might want to avoid Philadelphia County. Along with the District of Columbia, Philadelphia County is one of the worst places to live in the country—you only get 72.3 years.

Black Lung

The prevalence of a specific disease may vary a bit depending on the area, but very few are confined to just a few states. Pneumoconiosis is one of those diseases; it is limited to western Maryland, Virginia, West Virginia, Kentucky and... Pennsylvania. Miners make up 70 percent of the diagnosed cases of pneumoconiosis. Anyone who's lived in the coal country of eastern Pennsylvania can tell you about the miner's curse of black lung. Coal miner's pneumonoconiosis (CWP), more commonly known as black lung, does just what its nickname says. After years of breathing in the coal dust in and around mines, a miner's lungs become coated and turn black. Many families can tell you about grandfathers "on black lung"—the compensation provided by the Federal Coal Mine Health and Safety Act of 1969. Before that, miners who couldn't work because of the incessant coughing, shortness of breath and painful breathing caused by black lung were simply sent home by the largely unregulated coal industry. Increased federal regulations and health precautions have decreased the number of new cases of CWP, but the old miners aren't breathing any easier.

Got Drugs?

If you want drugs, Pennsylvania is the place to be—but in a good way. When you consider that tourists come to the state to step back in time to a place where automobiles share the roads with horses and buggies, it's hard to believe that industries come to the state to create cutting edge medical technology. Pennsylvania boasts 72,835 bioscience jobs that include medical research, development of drugs and pharmaceuticals, and creation of medical devices and equipment. In 2006, a whopping 1.4 billion dollars was awarded to medical researchers in the state by the National Institute of Health, much of it funneled to two universities: the University of Pennsylvania and the University of Pittsburgh. The alumni of another, the University of Sciences in Philadelphia, went on to become leaders in the pharmaceutical industry. Eight of the largest pharmaceutical companies in the United States are located in the state. Anyone who has visited a drugstore or doctor lately (or caught one of those ads touting the latest miracle drug) probably recognizes the names of several: Wyeth, GlaxoSmithKline, Johnson and Johnson, Merck, Pfizer and Cephalon.

Medical Marvels

Pennsylvania has been a leader in medical developments since the 1800s. Everyone who hates the taste of cough medicine (and every other liquid medicine) can thank a Pennsylvanian for the fact that most medications also come in pill form. Druggist Jacob Dunton was the first person in the United States to offer his customers the choice of "compressed pills," not the traditional nasty tasting liquids or powders they mixed with water before taking. But that was just the beginning of Pennsylvania's medical masterminding...

☛ Dr. Crawford Long was the first to use ether during surgery in 1842.

☛ Founded in 1904, the Fox Chase Cancer Center was the first hospital dedicated to cancer research. It was also the first to use radium to treat cancer.

☛ When Dr. Arthur Goodspeed invented the first x-ray photograph machine, he didn't want to try it on a human, so he x-rayed the coins in a purse instead.

☛ Dr. Jonas Salk discovered the polio vaccine on March 26, 1953. Until then, polio was highly contagious—just the year before Dr. Salk's discovery, there were nearly 60,000 cases and 3000 deaths in the U.S. alone. Public gathering places such as pools, beaches and carnivals were closed because people were afraid they would contract the disease. President Franklin D. Roosevelt, who led the country out of the Depression and through World War II, was confined to a wheelchair because of paralysis after contracting polio in 1921.

- Dr. Charles C. Chapple of Children's Hospital invented the nursery incubator in 1938.

- Pennsylvania wasn't done with vaccines. In 1963, Dr. Stanley A. Plotkin helped eradicate another deadly childhood disease with his German measles (ruebella) vaccine.

- And the Nobel Prize in Medicine goes to…Dr. Baruch S. Blumberg and Dr. Irving Millman for identifying the hepatitis B virus and developing the vaccine in 1967.

- The University of Pittsburgh Medical Center (UMPC) is renowned for its advances in transplant medicine, performing more than 12,000 transplants since 1981. UPMC developed an important anti-rejection drug as well as performing the world's first heart/liver transplant and the world's first heart/liver/kidney transplant.

COME TO PENNSYLVANIA—CAP AND GOWN INCLUDED

In Pennsylvania, you can't swing a cat without hitting a college or university. In fact, Pennsylvania is third on the list of states with the most colleges, just behind California and New York. Approximately 590,000 college students call the Keystone state home. We love education so much that many of our colleges don't stop at just one campus. The king of satellite campuses would have to be Pennsylvania State University or Penn State, which has about 80,000 students. The main campus, University Park, has 35,000 enrolled students. The other 45,000 are spread across the state at 19 other satellite campuses. The breakdown of Pennsylvania colleges and universities includes the following:

Private Four-Year Schools	86
State Universities	14
State Related Universities	4
Theological Seminaries	18
Two-Year Schools	8
Colleges of Technology	1

Harvard Shmarvard

Don't even mention the H-word at the University of Pennsylvania, better known as Penn. The ivy-league university in Philadelphia was established in 1740 with the help of Benjamin Franklin. After a few delays, classes started in 1751, and the facility was officially recognized by the state as a university in 1779. Remember that date—1779. Now Harvard may have started holding classes in 1636 (can one teacher and nine students really be called a school?) but it wasn't officially recognized by Massachusetts as a university until 1780. Penn recognized in 1779. Harvard recognized in 1780. Even someone from Harvard should be able to do the math. Penn is definitely the oldest university in the country.

If Harvard wants to argue about Penn's status as the nation's first university, that's fine; Penn has a few other records to its name:

☛ Nation's first school of medicine, established in 1765

☛ Nation's first teaching hospital, established in 1874

☛ World's first school of business—Wharton School—dates back to 1881

☛ Franklin Field, oldest collegiate football field still in use, first hosted a game in 1895

- Houston Hall, the first student union, which included a pool called the Houston Club Tank, established in 1896

- First double-decked college stadium, completed in 1925

- First female president of an Ivy League school—Judith Rodin—in 1994

First in Class

More firsts that Pennsylvanians could brag about (if we weren't so darned humble):

- Amos Neyhart was the world's bravest man. He was the country's first driver's ed teacher at State College Area High School in 1933.

- The first public school was established in Philadelphia in 1698.

- In 1850, Drexel University established the world's first medical school for women.

- The nation's first art institute was the Pennsylvania Academy of Fine Arts, established in 1805.

- The Carlisle Indian School was the first non-reservation school for Native Americans.

- The Institute of Colored Youth founded by Philadelphia Quaker Richard Humphreys was the first historically black college. Established in 1837, it later became Cheyney University.

- Famous for their support of education, the Quakers founded their first college, Haverford College, in 1833.

- The first rabbinic school in the United States, Maimonides College, was founded in 1867.

☛ Lincoln University became the first university to accept African students when 10 exchange students from Liberia enrolled in 1873.

☛ Carnegie Mellon is the only university to offer a degree in bagpipe music.

☛ In 1921, the first three African American women earned doctoral degrees. One of these, Sadie Tanner Mosell Alexander, received hers from University of Pennsylvania.

☛ In 1731, Benjamin Franklin organized the first shareholder library (members paid dues).

☛ Bryn Mawr, alma mater of Katherine Hepburn, was the nation's first school to offer graduate degrees in Social Work.

☛ The Penn State IFC/Panhellenic Dance Marathon (THON) is the largest student-run philanthropy in the world. The 46-hour dance marathon raises money for children's cancer. THON 2007 was a milestone; it was the first year the students raised more than 5 million dollars—$5,240,385.17 to be exact.

Schools in Philadelphia

More than 80,000 college students roam the city of Philadelphia and its suburbs at over 30 colleges including the following:

Villanova University
Founded: 1842 by the friars of the Order of St. Augustine
Town: Villanova
Chalkboard Trivia: It is the oldest and largest Catholic university in the state.

Temple University
Founded: 1884 by Dr. Russell Conwell
Town: Philadelphia
Chalkboard Trivia: They have campuses in Tokyo and Rome.

Drexel University

Founded: 1891 by Anthony Drexel

Town: Philadelphia

Chalkboard Trivia: Their mascot has been the Drexel Dragon since 1926, and his name is "Mario the Magnificent."

Schools Throughout the State

Many prestigious universities are located throughout the state.

Carnegie Mellon University

Founded: 1900 by Andrew Carnegie

Town: Pittsburgh

Chalkboard Trivia: The school is a magnet for Hollywood hopefuls—alums include Holly Hunter, Ted Danson, Judith Light, Blair Underwood, Steve Bochco and Laura San Giacomo.

Lehigh University

Founded: 1865 by Asa Packer

Town: Bethlehem

Chalkboard Trivia: In 1890, no tuition was charged.

Pennsylvania State University

Founded: 1855

Town: Campuses throughout the state

Chalkboard Trivia: The school mascot is called the "Nittany Lion" and the athletic teams the "Nittany Lions" after nearby Nittany Mountain. Folks thought the mountain was named after a Native American princess Nita-nee, but author Henry Shoemaker made her up in 1903.

University of Pittsburgh

Founded: 1787

Town: Pittsburgh

Chalkboard Trivia: The school started in a log cabin.

Got Milk?

One of Penn State's 160 majors is Food Science. What exactly Food Science entails is shrouded in mystery, but the important thing you should know is that it requires the university to have a herd of 225 cows and, consequently, about 4.5 million pounds (approximately 511,363 to 529,411 gallons) of milk a year. Now, no matter how much chocolate syrup you pour into it, you

aren't going to get the kids on the campus food plan to drink all that milk. Along came the Ice Cream Short Course—that was back in 1895. The result was the largest university creamery in the country. In 1896, the school began selling ice cream to an eager public, along with a bunch of other boring dairy products such as cheese, sour cream and, oh yeah, milk. But the important things are the ice cream, frozen yogurt and sherbet to the tune of 750,000 scoops a year—not including online sales. The Berkey Creamery (when you visit, just call it The Creamery) is not one to stick with the same old flavors and is constantly concocting new ones—some named after famous Penn State alumni or visitors. The most popular flavor is vanilla and the most unpopular (no longer available) was carrot. OK, what vegetarian suggested that?

The School Joke

One Pennsylvania school has been mentioned on at least four national television programs. It wasn't for a sports championship, an alumnus winning a Nobel Prize, or even for some crazy frat prank involving 16 guys, a keg of beer and a Volkswagen. It was becasue of the school's name. It all started in 1853 when a college was founded and named after the county in which it was located. Not so unusual, right? The name stuck even after the school was moved closer to Philadelphia. After all, it had had the name for decades. But then the school started getting national attention from the likes of David Letterman, Conan O'Brien, Howard Stern and Saturday Night Live, to name a few. Finally everyone agreed to toss tradition out the window. In 2001, Arcadia College was born, and Beaver College died a quiet but happily anticipated death. The tombstone reads "it seemed like a good idea at the time."

No Sex Ed Required

Pennsylvania law requires that everyone between the ages of 6 and 17 attend school, but every rule has its exceptions. This law's exception is a 1972 Supreme Court ruling that requires

Amish children to attend school from ages 6 until 14. Although some Amish children attend rural public school, 90 percent walk to a one- or two-room schoolhouse where the school day begins with an Amish teacher ringing a bell. According to the Pennsylvania Department of Education, there are 224 Amish schools in the state, with 216 located in Lancaster County alone. Although they speak Pennsylvania Dutch in their homes, lessons are taught in English (the teacher will sometime speak to first graders in German). The children learn history, math, geography, English and a little science. Religion, health and sex education are left to the parents. These schools have no electricity, and they use paper and pencils, not computers and calculators. Think Amish education is substandard? Although they aren't required to, Amish children who take standardized tests usually score above average. High school or college isn't forbidden for Amish children, either. For these higher levels, the Amish turn to the public school system.

What's Your Major?

At one Pennsylvania college, students don't have to worry about choosing a major, getting a date for the homecoming dance or getting caught drinking underage. So what school has only one major, no dances and a student body made up mostly of people in their forties? The U.S. Army War College (USAWC) at Carlisle Barracks. The word Army in the name is a bit misleading. For 55 years, Carlisle has been home to a school that welcomes military (all branches) and civilian leaders from all over the country as its students. Again, even though the name seems to spell it out—the school teaches war—the Army prefers to think of it as "teaching leadership." The school only has about 600 students at a time, some online and some living on "campus" (no frat houses here—just barracks). After 10 months (2 years if they're attending online) students get a Master's Degree in Strategic Studies.

POLITICAL MAKEUP

Pennsylvania is a swing state that is culturally conservative but economically liberal. They have 50 state senators and send 19 U.S. Representatives and 2 Senators to Washington DC.

Every Vote Counts

Speaking of presidential elections, Pennsylvania has long been the state without a voice. Its primary elections are in late April; more than 50 percent of the states hold their elections before Pennsylvania. Usually one candidate has secured enough delegate votes to be declared the party's nominee long before Pennsylvanians head for the polls. In the last 30 years, they have voted in only two elections when the nominee wasn't already chosen. In 1976, they helped chose Gerald Ford over Ronald Reagan in the Republican primary as well as Jimmy Carter over Sen. Henry Jackson, Congressman Morris Udall and George

Wallace in the Democratic primary. Both ultimately became their party's nominee, with Carter winning the election. In the 2008 primary between Democrats Hillary Rodham Clinton and Barack Obama, Pennsylvanians chose Clinton, who was strongly supported by Governor Ed Rendell and had family ties to Scranton. Despite the state's contribution of 21 electoral votes to Clinton, Barack Obama ultimately became the party's nominee.

Da, I Love Russian Winters

A graduate of Dickinson College, James Buchanan was a pretty experienced guy: five terms in the House of Representatives, Minister to Russia, 10 years in the Senate, Secretary of State for President James Polk and Minister to Great Britain for President Franklin Pierce. When the Democratic Party came knocking in 1856 and said "Hey Jim, wanna take a try at the presidency?" he decided to go for it. And he won. That's when it all hit the fan. It was slavery and states' rights all day, every day. Cabinet members were resigning, the Southern and Northern congressmen managed to stalemate every vote in Congress, and the Democratic Party was split. Those cold Russian winters were beginning to look pretty good to our 15th president. Buchanan kept a low profile during the presidential election of 1860, which included Republican lawyer Abraham Lincoln, Constitutional Union nominee John Bell and two Democrats. The official Democratic nominee was Stephen Douglas, but the Southern Democrats, calling themselves the National Democrats, backed John Breckinridge. Even though Buchanan left the White House in March of 1861 and the secessionists didn't fire on Fort Sumter until April of that year, his legacy became "the guy who started the Civil War". Most historians believe the Civil War was inevitable, but the events leading up to it happened on Buchanan's watch. Because of this, the "Buchanan effect" was said to influence Pennsylvania politicians for generations, keeping them from the most sought-after spots in national government. Decision makers behind the scenes didn't want to risk getting another Buchanan.

DID YOU KNOW?

Buchanan's also in the record books as the only president from Pennsylvania and the only president to remain a bachelor. Theories abound about the reasons for his confirmed bachelorhood—the official line is that his heart was broken when his fiancé Ann Coleman called off the wedding. Others say Buchanan worked both sides of the aisle (and they don't mean Republicans and Democrats).

The First First Lady

Because James Buchanan was a bachelor, his niece Harriet Lane filled the roll of as hostess for "Nunc" during his White House years. In 1860, the magazine *Frank Leslie's Illustrated Monthly* referred to her as "the Lady of the White House, and by courtesy, the First Lady of the Land." It was the first written reference to the First Lady, and the title stuck. In fact, most state governments and many other nations adopted this American creation.

DID YOU KNOW?

After completing his second term as President in 1961, Dwight D. Eisenhower and his wife Mamie retired to a farm in Gettysburg. Although he was raised in Texas, Eisenhower attended West Point and served in the Army until he was elected President. After a lifetime in Army housing—and the White House—the Gettysburg farm was the first home the Eisenhowers owned.

The Man Who Would Be...Everything

Although he was born in Boston in 1706, Benjamin Franklin moved to Philadelphia as a young man. With the exception of brief periods of time in London and France, he lived in Pennsylvania until his death at age 84, in 1790. It hardly seems fair to categorize Franklin as just a politician, inventor, scientist,

writer or musician. He was all that and more. Everyone remembers that Benjamin Franklin was the guy who conducted primitive electricity experiments with a kite and a key. But if that's all you know, you're missing a lot. When you look at a list of Benjamin Franklin's accomplishments, it hardly seems possible that one man did them all.

- ☞ Creator of a Nation: the only person to sign all four documents that helped create the United States (Declaration of Independence; Treaty of Alliance with France; Treaty of Peace between England, France and United States; and Constitution)

- ☞ Ambassador: to France

- ☞ Inventions: bifocals, lightning rod (got tired of flying the kite, I guess), Franklin Stove, odometer

- ☞ Medicine: invented flexible urinary catheter and co-founded the nation's first hospital, Pennsylvania Hospital, with Dr. Thomas Bond in 1751

- Fire Safety: established the first fire company, Union Fire Company, in 1736 and the first fire insurance

- Author: the "Pennsylvania Gazette" and "Poor Richard's Almanack" (where he made the first printed weather forecasts) and the book *Experiments and Observations on Electricity*

- President: of Pennsylvania (precursor to the position of Governor), American Philosophical Society and Pennsylvania Society for Promoting the Abolition of Slavery

- Musician: played the violin, harp, guitar and armonica (a glass instrument played by touching spinning glass—if you want to know what it sounds like, think Sandra Bullock playing the water glasses in *Miss Congeniality*)

- And in his spare time: helped established a paper currency system in the U.S., set up the first Circulating Library in the country, set up Postal Service for Philadelphia and charted the Gulf Stream

If you would not be forgotten, as soon as you are dead and rotten, either write things worth reading or do things worth the writing.
–Benjamin Franklin

Governor Thomas Mifflin

The first elected governor of Pennsylvania (1790–99) was a key figure not only in the history of Pennsylvania but in the creation of a new nation. A wealthy businessman, Thomas Mifflin came into contact with men such as Benjamin Franklin and Samuel Adams, both socially and as a Philadelphia city warden and member of the colonial legislature. The influence of these men (as well as the negative influence of increasing British taxes on his wallet) encouraged Mifflin to be a member of both the First and Second Continental Congresses. During the Second Congress, he resigned to join the Army—a move that got him expelled from the Quaker Church. After four years in the Army, he returned to political life in 1779 (who wouldn't after a winter at Valley Forge?). While Mifflin was serving as President of the Second Continental Congress, General George Washington resigned his military commission to President Mifflin before being sworn in as the President and Commander in Chief. Mifflin was appointed Pennsylvania's President of Council (a fancy way of saying governor) for two years before a new state constitution called for the first election of a governor. He won and remained governor for nine years. Like many of the men who ran our country, Mifflin wasn't that great at balancing a budget—he died penniless, and the country paid for his burial.

DID YOU KNOW?

The first Secretary of the Homeland Security Office after 9-11 was Tom Ridge from Erie who served as governor from 1995 to 2001.

Pennsylvanians Who've Contributed to the History Books

Henry "Hap" Arnold	U.S. Army and U.S. Air Force General
Smedley Butler	U.S. Marine Corps General
James J. Davis	U.S. Secretary of Labor, U.S. Senator
George M. Dallas	11th Vice President
Newt Gingrich	Speaker of the House
Winfield Scott Hancock	Union commander
George Marshall	U.S. Army General (World War II), Secretary of State
Tom Ridge	First Secretary of Homeland Security (1995–2001)
Dick Thornburgh	U.S. Attorney General (1979–87)

Thank Goodness She's Finally Getting Married

When Cornelia Bryce announced she was getting married at the ripe old age of 33, her family was relieved. Not only had this daughter of a wealthy New York congressman refused to make her debut (horrors!), she was a suffragette (gasp!). After Cornelia's marriage on August 15, 1914, to Gifford Pinchot, the first chief of the U.S. Forest Service and a candidate in the race for Pennsylvania Representative, the family envisioned lady-like teas in Cornelia's future. Boy, were they wrong! She kept up her wild ways—marching in suffrage parades and labor union picket lines, especially those that had female members. Even when her husband was elected governor of Pennsylvania (he served from 1923–26 and 1931–34) Cornelia continued fighting for social reform, considered only second to that rabble-rouser Eleanor Roosevelt. The governor even appointed her to a state-wide commission to investigate sweatshops—factory owners branded her "an agitator and strike leader." After World War II, Cornelia had a new issue to fight for: international disarmament and government control of uranium ore. She may have never held an elected office (not that she didn't try—she ran three times for the Republican U.S. Congressional seat) but Cornelia Bryce Pinchot influenced the country in many ways.

Slavery In Pennsylvania

Most people are surprised to learn that slavery existed in Pennsylvania from the 1600s, reaching its peak in the 1750s, when there were approximately 6000 slaves in the colony. But, as long as there were slaves in the state, there were also abolitionist groups. Many Quakers or "Friends" protested against the bondage of human beings and, in 1688, four Germantown Quakers issued the first written protest of slavery. Pennsylvanians continued to object to slavery and, in 1775, formed the Society for the Relief of Free Negroes Unlawfully held in Bondage. Better known as the Pennsylvania Abolition Society, it was the first organization against slavery in the nation.

The state government began to take notice of the public's view and began taxing the slave trade in the 1700s, hoping to prevent its growth. In 1780, the Pennsylvania Assembly passed the first legislative act against slavery: the Act for the Gradual Abolition of Slavery. Of course "gradual" is the key word—an owner didn't have to free his slaves until they reached the age of 28. The Pennsylvania Abolition Society bought and immediately freed as many slaves as they could. By 1850, there were no slaves in Pennsylvania. By comparison, Virginia had over 1.4 million slaves and 472,000 citizens in the same year.

All Aboard! Next Stop Freedom

The town of Columbia may have been the first Underground Railroad station to exist. Just north of the Maryland border, it had a large settlement of freed slaves and became a prime spot for slaves from nearby Virginia and Maryland to disappear. Slaves seeking freedom in Canada often went through Pennsylvania, but the Underground Railroad was not a well-organized group. Most people who aided fugitives were anonymous, and each knew only enough to tell their visitors where to go next. Helpers on the Underground Railroad were often religious people, especially Quakers. They hid and fed the fugitives before sending them on to another friendly home. Another key part of the Underground Railroad was the almost 56,000 free African Americans in the state by the 1850s. One of the leaders in aiding fugitive slaves was Robert Purvis, a Philadelphia African American and businessman. In 1837, he organized the Vigilant Society of Philadelphia, which not only helped slaves escape but also provided clothes, cash and other necessities. No one knows how many fugitives were aided by Pennsylvanians or how many stops on the Underground Railroad were located throughout the state.

BEAUTIFUL AND DECORATIVE

Just for Fancy

The Pennsylvania Dutch are known for being practical and simple. But many of the habits and traditions that they regard as part of everyday life are art in the eyes of "the English." Their art isn't confined to frames hanging on a wall. It is everywhere, including the barns in counties such as Lancaster, Berks and Bucks. Most barns are decorated by traditional hex signs—patterns painted on the side of the barn. Usually these patterns are eight-sided stars contained within a circle painted in primary colors. Hex signs began in the Old Country as a way of warding off evil spirits, but the Pennsylvania Dutch will assure you that nowadays they are "just for fancy" or for decoration. The hex signs, sometimes very complicated and beautiful, have intrigued visitors for years. Because not every Pennsylvania tourist has a barn at home that they can adorn with a hex sign, the symbols can be found on everything from dish towels to T-shirts to salt and pepper shakers.

Sewing Circles

Quilting, which was once an opportunity to blend the practical task of sewing with a social visit to friends and neighbors, has become a way for many Pennsylvania Dutch women to supplement their family's income. Although they are accustomed to the hundreds of dollars their quilts now fetch, they are probably still amazed by the fact that many of the quilts will not be used to keep a loved one warm on a snowy night, but will instead be hung on a wall, displayed like a work of art. Even when quilting was a way to put scraps of materials or worn out clothing to use, the results were beautiful with patterns such as Star of Bethlehem, Wedding Ring, Turkey Tracks, Tree of Paradise or Seven Stars. The leftovers scraps of cloth from yesteryear have been replaced by fine materials, now that the admiration of the outside world has raised this household task to an art.

Keystone Calligraphy

Today's brides view wedding invitations addressed in calligraphy as the height of sophistication. How surprised they would be if they knew that the decidedly unsophisticated Pennsylvania Dutch have been practicing their own version of calligraphy, called *fraktur,* for hundreds of years. In addition to elaborate lettering, they also use illustrations such as animals, angels and trees to create unique certificates to commemorate occasions such as births, baptisms, marriages and house blessings.

Clip Art

Have you ever folded up a piece of paper and cut out pieces with scissors—creating a snowflake? If so, you can imagine the art of *scherenschnitte* (sharon-sh-net) or scissor cutting—but just barely. The Pennsylvania Dutch aren't satisfied with a simple, symmetrical snowflake. Their cuttings are elaborate creations that include hearts, birds and flowers or are even entire scenes, such as a bride and groom dancing or animals marching into Noah's ark. They are often used as Valentines or to decorate important documents such as wedding certificates. The cuttings are usually done on white paper and then mounted on a darker color. Rumor has it that bored shepherds started the art form using the scissors meant for shearing sheep.

Soup as Art

Before he was Andy Warhol (1928–87), king of Pop Art, he was Andrew Warhola, the son of Slovak immigrants in Pittsburgh. After graduating from the Carnegie Institute of Technology in Pittsburgh in 1949, Andy headed for the Big Apple, where we can only assume he was very hungry because much of his art focused on food—Campbell's Soup cans, Coke bottles, ice cream, even bananas. Then he moved on to silk-screened images of famous people, such as Marilyn Monroe, Elvis Presley and Jackie Onassis. The Andy Warhol Museum that opened in Pittsburgh in 1994 contains more than 4000 of his works and is the largest museum dedicated solely to one artist.

Hanging Out at the Philadelphia Museum of Art

Tom Gralish and Michael Vitez spent a year at the Philadelphia Museum of Art. They must really love art! Actually, they never went inside the museum (ok, maybe a few times to use the bathroom). Instead, they hung out on the steps. Why? Because these were THE steps—the ones Rocky ran up. And Rocky Balboa/ Sylvester Stallone wasn't the only one; everyday somebody decides to re-enact Rocky's triumph—Japanese tourists, immigrants who just took their citizen's oath, guys about to ask their girlfriends to marry them (hey, not my choice for a romantic proposal but...). The Pulitzer Prize winning photographer and writer compiled the best runs into a book called *Rocky Stories: Tales of Love, Hope and Happiness at America's Most Famous Steps.*

Pennsylvania Artists

Andrew and N.C. Wyeth (Chadds Ford)

George Catlin (Wilkes-Barre)

Mary Cassat (Allegheny City)

Thomas Eakin (Philadelphia)

Benjamin West (Springfield)

THE WRITTEN AND SPOKEN WORD

Local Boy Makes Good—Town Horrified
The country loved the scandalous tales John O'Hara wrote in his short stories and novels, such as "Appointment at Samarra" and *Ten North Frederick*. Everyone, that is, except the people who felt that his characters were thinly disguised versions of themselves and their neighbors (a little too thinly disguised, some might say). Even though O'Hara altered the names of towns and businesses of the area where he grew up, the residents of Schuylkill County weren't fooled. Of course O'Hara's Gibbsville was actually Pottsville, and that drunken spinster in his *New Yorker* story was Aunt Minnie. Even though his work was tremendously popular, earned awards and was made into movies such as *Butterfield 8* (starring Elizabeth Taylor), *From the Terrace* (starring Paul Newman) and *Pal Joey* (starring Frank Sinatra) many residents decided to ignore his success. In fact, his books were banned from some local libraries and kept behind the counter in others.

But time heals all wounds. Or could it be that all the infamous characters of his books have died? Today, not only do the local libraries have all of O'Hara's works on their shelves, but the county celebrates O'Hara Days each October.

The Patriarch of Reality Television

The first national show that was a mash-up of live TV performances and soap opera drama was *American Bandstand*, straight out of Philly. It started in 1952 as a local show hosted by popular disc jockey Bob Horn. Unfortunately, celebrities are the same whether it's 1956 or 2006. In 1956, Horn was arrested for DUI and was replaced by 26-year-old, clean-cut Dick Clark. The show became so popular with the new host that, the following year, it went national, five afternoons a week. Teenagers tuned in for the music, the dancing and the romances between the dancers from local high schools, until 1964 when Dick headed for a sunnier coast—California. But the building at 4601 Market Street was awarded a historical marker in 1997 to commemorate *American Bandstand* and for the fact that "this 1947 building was one of the first designed and constructed exclusively for television productions." *American Bandstand,* which ran until 1987, spawned shows like *Sump'n Else, Soul Train* and *Disco America*. It was also fictionalized in the TV series *American Dreams,* the movie *The In-Crowd*, and most recently in *Hairspray* (one Broadway show and two movies).

Capturing Pennsylvania On Screen

Rocky wasn't the only Pennsylvanian movie or TV show to capture America's attention. Although the most recognizable cities—Philadelphia and Pittsburgh—are the stars of many television series and movies other lesser known sites such as Harrisburg, Scranton and Valley Forge have also had their 15 minutes of fame.

All the Right Moves	*National Treasure*
Animal House	*Philadelphia*
Boy Meets World	*Signs*
Cold Case	*The Blob*
Flashdance	*The Deer Hunter*
Gettysburg	*The Molly Maguires*
Girl, Interrupted	*The Office*
Groundhog Day	*The Philadelphia Story*
It's Always Sunny in Philadelphia	*The Sixth Sense*
My So-Called Life	*Thirtysomething*
	Witness

MUM'S THE WORD

Real Men Do Wear Feathers

Not everyone can wear feathers—Zsa Zsa Gabor, Carrie Bradshaw, guys from South Philly... Although the face of South Philly is changing, it is still a neighborhood of immigrants. A hundred years ago, the newcomers were from Italy, Ireland and Poland—today they come from many more countries: Cambodia, China, Haiti, India, Russia, Thailand. But it's the original families that called South Philly home that wear the feathers. Not every day—364 days a year they wear the clothes of cops, firefighters, electricians and truck drivers. But the first day of the year, they take some time to "strut their stuff."

Explaining how a mummer struts is like explaining how a bird flies—impossible for the average person. Mere words can never truly explain the reality, but www.mummers.com gives it a shot:

To approximate the Mummers' strut, you spread your arms, supporting an invisible cape; pumping your elbows, rocking and bobbing your body, you strut forward and back, sideways and in circles; all the way along the line of march.

Try it. I dare you. Now imagine doing this in front of 30,000 of your neighbors—while wearing feathers. Being a mummer is not for the faint of heart.

Birth of the Mummers

Mummery (probably taken from a German word meaning disguise) is an ancient tradition that dates back to Roman festivals from 400 BC honoring Saturnalias. Immigrants brought traditions for welcoming the new year from their own countries to Philadelphia, everything from shooting off guns and noise-making to scare away demons to visiting homes in costume to ensure good luck. All these traditions combined to create that unique celebration—the Mummers' Parade. Picture huge, dancing human peacocks with a dash of humor, catchy music and a lot of high-spirited attitude. Mummers were strutting in the streets of Philadelphia as early as the American Revolution, when their reward was food and drink from the audience of amused neighbors. The first official parade was in 1901, when prizes worth $1725 were offered. It has since grown to an eight-hour parade up Broad Street to City Hall. Mummer fans can also enjoy musical and dancing performances by the Fancy Brigade clubs—the most extravagant type of mummers—in the city's Pennsylvania Convention Center. Think Las Vegas meets Broadway musical with a touch of the circus tossed in. In a century of performing, the parade has only been postponed 22 times and cancelled twice—once in 1919 because of World War I and again in 1934 because of the Great Depression.

Time to Strut Your Stuff

The parade of 10,000 performers has four divisions—comics, fancies, string bands and fancy brigades. Within each division there are clubs that perform together every year. Although they only strut one day a year, the members of the clubs spend the other 364 days deciding on their theme, designing costumes, practicing their routines and raising money. Some clubs offer sneak peeks of their routines, but the costumes themselves are the best kept secret in Philly, only revealed as the mummers come strutting down Broad Street. The costumes, which once might have been sewn by the wives and mothers of the mummers, are now so ornate they demand professional costumers and can cost thousands of dollars. According to Steve Coper of

the Fralinger String Band, the average 64-piece string band can cost between $30,000 and $80,000 to costume each year. String bands aren't just about costumes, they also play music using accordions, violins, banjoes, saxophones and percussion instruments (but no brass instruments). Each year clubs choose a theme for their performance. For instance, the year the King Tut exhibit visited Philly, plenty of clubs were strutting as mummies with pyramid- and sphinx-shaped floats and props. The comics are recognized, not for red noses and big shoes, but for their parasols and traditional mummers' song "Oh Dem Golden Slippers." As they strut down the street, the comics poke fun at everything from celebrities to politicians to recent scandals.

For some people New Year's Day is about resolutions, hangovers or family dinners. In Pennsylvania, it's about feathers, strutting and humming along to the mummers' marches.

BIRTHPLACE: PENNSYLVANIA

Lights, Camera, Action

Many Pennsylvanians have been tempted by the lure of the stage lights in neighboring New York. From there it's just a quick airplane ride to the magic of Hollywood. Our state has contributed gifted artists on both sides of the camera to create the movies and TV shows we all love.

Kevin Bacon (Philadelphia)

Ethel, John and Lionel Barrymore (Philadelphia)

Danny Bonaduce (Broomall)

Charles Bronson (Ehrenfeld)

Tina Fey (Upper Darby)

W.C. Fields (Philadelphia)

Richard Gere (Philadelphia)

Jeff Goldblum (Pittsburgh)

Michael Keaton (Pittsburgh)

Grace Kelly—Princess Grace of Monaco (Philadelphia)

Jack Klugman (Philadelphia)

Jayne Mansfield (Bryn Mawr)

Dennis Miller (Pittsburgh)

Jack Palance (Hazle Township)

William Powell (Pittsburgh)

Fred Rogers (Latrobe)

Bob Saget (Philadelphia)

David O. Selznick (Pittsburgh)

M. Night Shyamalan (Philadelphia)

Will Smith (Philadelphia)

Sharon Stone (Meadville)

Jonathon Taylor Thomas (Bethlehem)

Did They Start Out With the Pennsylvania Polka?

Pennsylvanians don't just enjoy the polka. Who knew that the old favorite "the twist" was a Pennsylvania export? Rap, swing, jazz, punk, rock, hair bands, boy bands and opera all have gifted artists with Pennsylvanian roots.

Christina Aguilera (Pittsburgh)

Marian Anderson (Philadelphia)

Frankie Avalon (Philadelphia)

Bill Haley and His Comets (Upland)

Boyz II Men (Philadelphia)

Fabian/Fabiano Bonaparte (Philadelphia)

Breaking Benjamin (Wilkes Barre)

Chubby Checker (Philadelphia)

Perry Como (Canonsburg)

Jim Croce (Drexel Hill)

DJ Jazzy Jeff (Philadelphia)

Tommy and Jimmy Dorsey (Shenandoah)

Kevin Eubanks (Philadelphia)

Hall and Oates (Pottstown)

The Hooters (Philadelphia)

Joan Jett (Philadelphia)

Jay Livingston (McDonald)

Pink/Alecia Moore (Doylestown)

Poison (Doylestown)

Bobby Vinton (Canonsburg)

Author, Author

Whereas some authors have introduced Pennsylvania to their readers through their writing, others have traveled the world, and their writing reflects it. The works of Pennsylvanian authors have brought Pacific islands, Poland, Mexico and even Russia alive for their readers.

Louisa May Alcott (Germantown)

Steven Vincent Benét (Bethlehem)

Nelly Bly (Apollo)

Willa Cather (Pittsburgh)

Joseph Heller (State College)

Dean Kootz (Everett)

James Michener (Doylestown)

John O'Hara (Pottsville)

Conrad Richter (Pine Grove)

Lisa Scottoline (Philadelphia)

Martin Cruz Smith (Reading)

Gertrude Stein (Allegheny)

Wallace Stevens (Reading)

John Updike (Reading)

INVENTIONS, TECHNOLOGIES & CREATIONS

Any Requests?

If you've ever switched on the radio during your commute to work or to drown out the fighting of your precious children in the backseat, you can thank a Pennsylvanian: Frank Conrad— engineer at Westinghouse Electric Company by day, ham operator in his Pittsburgh garage by night. Conrad built a ham radio in 1916 and may have spent the rest of his days chatting with other ham operators if he hadn't decided to play a few records on the air. Other operators began sending him song requests. Horne's Department Store even began selling receivers using Conrad's broadcasts as a selling point.

Harry Davis, Vice President of Westinghouse, convinced Conrad to build a more powerful transmitter and apply for commercial status. In 1920, Conrad began broadcasting as the first commercial radio station, with the call letters KDKA. The station started with a bang—reporting the election returns for the Presidential election between James Cox and Warren Harding on November 2.

Naturally, KDKA achieved plenty of firsts.

- First professional radio announcer—Leo Rosenberg

- First remote broadcast—Church service on Jan. 2, 1921

- First sporting event—Championship prizefight on April 11, 1921

- First baseball game broadcast—Pirates game on August 2, 1921

Things didn't always go smoothly. The station was located near a railroad track—every evening at 8:30, listeners were treated to the sound of a freight train whistle. Once a singer had her performance at the station interrupted when she swallowed a bug mid-warble. And because they couldn't set up a remote broadcast inside the baseball stadium, the operators used a relay method. One guy would buy a ticket and settle into a seat near the fence. As plays happened he would jot them down and drop the updates over the fence to a second man. He ran the papers to a third guy across the street who was in contact with the station via a public telephone. Finally the news would reach the station and the listeners. But the listeners mustn't have minded the short delay—they're still listening almost a century later, making KDKA the longest continually broadcasting radio station.

Additions to the Toy Box

Most inventors start with a problem and invent the solution. And then there are the inventors who find themselves with an interesting doo-dad and say, "What can I do with this?" Two of those men were Richard James and Earl L. Warrick.

It's traespiral, it's traespiral, for fun it's a wonderful toy…
Richard James was just minding his own business when inspiration hit. Specifically, he was a naval engineer doing an experiment when a tension spring fell off a shelf. As it bounced across the floor, James forgot about battleships and started thinking about toy boxes. While James spent two years deciding what wire gauge and coil had the most bounce, his wife, Betty, was assigned the job of coming up with the perfect name. Paging through the dictionary she discovered *slinky,* a Swedish word meaning "traespiral" or "sleek and sinuous."

Finally, during the Christmas season of 1945, they were ready to unveil the Slinky at a demonstration at Gimbel's Department Store in Philadelphia. Richard was so nervous he convinced a friend to be a "plant" and stand in the crowd to stir up interest and buy the first Slinky. The plant couldn't get near enough to the table to buy one—all 400 Slinkies sold out in 90 minutes. With $500, the James' started the James Spring and Wire Company.

More than 60 years later, equipment Richard designed is still twisting 80 feet of wire into a Slinky at the Hollidaysburg factory. At last count, over 300 million Slinkies have been sold—and all because a spring fell off a shelf.

Squishy Fun

Earl L. Warrick, a Butler native, received a doctorate from Carnegie Mellon University in 1943 and then, like any promising scientist of the time, joined the war effort. He was working for Dow Corning when he combined a silicone derivative with boric acid. He wanted a substitute for rubber, but what he got was an elastic substance that didn't seem to be good for anything. Warrick and fellow scientist Rob Roy McGregor each received a $1 bonus from Dow for the 1943 patent for this bouncing putty and basically forgot about it. Warrick and his group of scientists went on to invent silicone rubber, used for underwater masks and automotive tubing; silicon, used in computer microchips; and a lubricant to help gears operate smoothly. After 30 years with Dow, Warrick was named on 44 patents. But it was Peter Hodgson of New Haven, Connecticut, who dubbed the useless invention Silly Putty, popped it in a plastic egg and became a millionaire. Upon his death, Warrick's daughter Cathy said her father was amused by the success of his scientific failure as a child's toy.

DID YOU KNOW?

Earl L. Warrick isn't the only scientist to claim to be the inventor of the material that became Silly Putty. Both Earl L. Warrick and James Wright, a General Electric scientist, claimed to have invented it in the year 1943 but, because Warrick received his patent first, most consider him the official inventor.

Invented in Pennsylvania

1858—Hymen L. Lipman received a patent for gluing an eraser to a pencil—they were always separate before that. The Faber Pencil Company developed a different way to attach erasers and Lipman sued. The case went to the U.S. Supreme Court, where Lipman's patent was revoked after the court said, "...to be patentable, [a product] must produce a different force or effect."

1866—Christopher Sholes, a mechanical engineer from Moorseburg, invented the first practical typewriter along with his partners S. W. Soule and G. Glidden. After the three men spent five years working out the kinks, their invention was manufactured by Remington Arms Company. Sholes foolishly sold his share of the patent to James Densmore (of QWERTY fame) and never reaped the financial rewards of the invention.

1888—Theophilus Van Kannel from Philadelphia invented the revolving door because he was sick and tired of holding doors open for perfectly capable women. He even installed them in the inner doorways of his and his mother's homes so he wouldn't always be jumping up to hold doors for his wife and mother.

1889—Joshua Pusey, a Philadelphia lawyer and cigar smoker, was embarrassed to go to fancy events with wooden kitchen matches sticking out of his pocket. He invented paper matches, but they didn't catch on until he convinced the Mendelsohn Opera Company to advertise their New York opening by printing their name on books of matches in 1897. Apparently opera lovers also use a lot of matches. Pusey eventually sold the patent to Diamond Match Company for $4000.

1893—The World's Fair was being held in Chicago and the fair committee wanted something to rival Paris' Eiffel Tower, unveiled at the World Fair in 1889. George W. Ferris, a Pittsburgh bridge builder, after listening to complaints during an engineers' dinner that nothing suitable had yet been found, had a brainstorm, that he scribbled on his napkin. The Ferris wheel amazed fair attendees. For 50 cents, brave visitors could enter one of 36 cars that held up to 60 people each. During the fair, the wheel earned $726,805.50 and the respect of engineers around the world.

WHY WE DO THE THINGS WE DO

Sitting on the Lazy Board

Ever wonder why Americans drive on the right side of the road? Perhaps because we didn't want to imitate our arch enemy, the British? Or maybe it's because, in the U.S., steering wheels are located on the left side of cars? Could it be that some anonymous bureaucrat tossed a coin when he was writing the road rules? Wrong, wrong, wrong. Strangely enough, you can thank a group of Pennsylvanians that don't even drive (cars, that is)—the Amish.

Although they preferred the old ways, the Amish were perfectly willing to invent things that made their work easier. One of those things was the Conestoga wagon. Invented in the 1750s, the boat-shaped wagon was pulled by 6 to 8 horses and was used to carry loads from Amish farms to town. These big wagons were eventually responsible for relocating half the country after a newspaper editor incited the public with his quote "Go West, young man!" Although drivers often walked alongside their horses, these wagons also had a "lazy board" on the left-hand side, where a driver could sit and still operate the brake. Conestoga wagons were big, and colonial roads were small, so when two vehicles met on the road and one of them was a Conestoga wagon, a bit of squeezing was involved. Sitting on their lazy boards, drivers of Conestoga wagons naturally veered to the right so they could better keep an eye on how close they were coming to the approaching vehicle. Not wanting to be crushed to a pulp, other drivers got into the habit of driving on the right also.

So, in 1792, when the Pennsylvania legislature was passing laws regarding the nation's first turnpike, from Lancaster to Philadelphia, lawmakers took their cue from the Amish and decreed that turnpike traffic should travel on the right. And—as with so many other things—as Pennsylvania goes, so goes the nation (and $2/3$ of the world—66 percent of nations require their drivers to travel on the right side of the road).

DID YOU  KNOW?

Because they were so large, Conestoga wagons were equipped with strings of bells as a warning to other travelers. Tradition was, if you got stuck and had to be helped by another vehicle, you gave that driver your team bells. You couldn't wear bells again until you had helped a driver in need. When trying to assure their wives they wouldn't be in any mishaps on the road, Conestoga wagon drivers would tell their wives not to worry, they would "be there with bells on."

So a Buggy and a Chevy Come to an Intersection…

It's not a joke. It's reality for many Pennsylvanians, especially in Lancaster County, where a bearded man and bonneted woman traveling to a neighboring farm or into town in their box-shaped buggy is a familiar sight. You could easily mistake them for time travelers from 300 years ago if it wasn't for one little thing…the neon orange triangle attached to the back of each buggy. The state requires that slow moving or difficult to see vehicles display a warning triangle. The Amish buggies—traveling at 3 to 10 miles per hour and painted black—qualify for the ordinance on both counts. Although the Amish are wary of symbols (including orange safety triangles), most have bowed to this "English" rule in the name of safety.

Amish Rules of the Road

Even though they do not require a state driver's license to drive a horse and buggy, members of the Amish community collaborated with the Pennsylvania Department of Transportation and State Police to write the "Horse and Buggy Driver's Manual." Along with horse and buggy safety, basic instructions included in a traditional Driver's Manual are quaintly expressed:

☛ It is our Christian duty to always practice the Golden Rule and not "hog" the road.

☛ It can be very worrisome to other drivers to see arms and legs dangling out of doors and windows. Drivers behind you are concerned that someone may fall out of the buggy and get hit by the driver.

☛ It is foolish and dangerous to insist upon one's right-of-way. The engraving on a tombstone illustrates this very well:

Here lies the body of William Gray
He died preserving his right-of-way
He was right (dead right) as he sped along
But he's just as dead as if he had been wrong.

I bet Mr. Gray wished they had finished the Horse and Buggy Driver's Manual before his last (and I do mean LAST) buggy ride.

KRAZY KRIMES IN THE KEYSTONE STATE

It is illegal to have more than 16 women living in a house together because that constitutes a brothel.

It is illegal to sleep on top of a refrigerator outdoors.

You cannot catch fish with dynamite or any part of your body except your mouth.

It is prohibited to talk loudly at picnics.

You may not sing in the bathtub.

Housewives may not hide dirt or dust under a rug.

Juggling in front of an airplane is illegal.

If a driver sees a team of horses, he must pull to one side of the road and cover his machine with a blanket or dust cover that has been painted to blend in with the scenery.

No man may buy alcohol without written permission from his wife.

You cannot discharge a gun, cannon, revolver or other explosive weapon at a wedding.

It's against the law to put a dollar on a string on the ground and yank it away when someone tries to pick it up.

MISBEHAVING PENNSYLVANIANS

Prisons Aplenty

Pennsylvania takes second place for the state with the most prisons, right behind Texas. According to the Federal Bureau of Prisons there are 14 federal facilities and 27 state correctional institutes.

The Blacksmith Did It

Patrick Lyon was simply a blacksmith that didn't want to catch the yellow fever spreading throughout Philadelphia in the summer of 1798. So he decided to head for Delaware with his apprentice. Just before he left, he did one last job—changing the fittings and locks on two iron vault doors. Unfortunately, those locks were in the Bank of Pennsylvania, and soon afterward the bank was robbed of $162,821—America's first bank robbery. The cops called it an inside job and the man they were looking for was Pat Lyon. Yellow fever epidemic or not, Lyon headed back to Philadelphia shouting, "It wasn't me! It was that carpenter working in the bank at the same time, Samuel Robinson." Close but no cigar—it was actually a friend of Robinson's named Isaac Davis and an unknown partner working with the bank's porter Thomas Cunningham. Cunningham might never have been caught if he hadn't started depositing the money he stole into the very same bank he stole it from. Cunningham's partners had died of yellow fever but he returned the money and never served any prison time.

Patrick Lyon wasn't so lucky. He spent three months in Walnut Street Prison—where he caught yellow fever. After he was released, an annoyed Lyon spent his free time writing a book about his experience and suing the city for false imprisonment. He was awarded $12,000—several years worth of salary for a blacksmith.

PHENOMENAL PENNSYLVANIA The first manned balloon in the United States was launched from Walnut Street Prison. The 1793 flight by Francois Jean Pierre Blanchard was not The Great Escape: Air Style. Instead, the balloon took off from the prison because Blanchard was worried that the enthusiastic crowds would accidentally puncture his balloon. Thankfully, President George Washington provided the Frenchman with a written "passport." Blanchard landed 15 miles away in a New Jersey farm field, the owners of which knew nothing of balloons or Blanchard's language—French. A swig from Blanchard's flask and the familiar name "George Washington" on his passport soothed the pitchfork-wielding and gun-toting farmers alarmed by this alien who dropped down from the sky.

Molly Maguires: Murderers or Heroes?

The Molly Maguires story is a confusing one; it is hard to separate fact from fiction. This much is known. In the 1870s, there were no unions to protect coal miners in eastern Pennsylvania. The mine owners dictated what was done, including the actions of the police. The miners may not have had a union, but they did have a few organizations on their side: the Workingman's Benevolent Association (WBA), which pressed for fair working conditions; and the Association of the Ancient Hibernians (AOH) a social club for Irish Americans. This is where things get a little fuzzy. Many people believe that a third group was also working behind the scenes for workers' rights—the Molly Maguires, a secret society of Irish-Americans fighting the unfair edicts of the mine owners. When the miners went on strike in 1875, Franklin Gowen, president of the Philadelphia and Reading Coal and Iron Company, hired Pinkerton agent James McParlan to infiltrate the Mollies and learn their plans. Twenty miners were ultimately hung in Pottsville and Mauch Chunk for murder and other crimes. But it seems the trials left more questions than they answered. To this day, it is not clear whether there actually was a Molly Maguire organization or whether it was just a myth and the hanged miners just scapegoats.

PHENOMENAL PENNSYLVANIA

When the sheriff came to take him to his hanging, Alexander Campbell—an accused Molly Maguire who had always maintained his innocence—placed his hand on the wall of his Mauch Chunk (now known as Jim Thorpe) jail cell and said, "There is proof of my words. That mark of mine will NEVER be wiped out. It will remain forever to shame the county for hanging an innocent man." An eerie handprint remained on the wall despite various sheriffs' efforts to remove it by cleaning, repainting and even tearing down the wall and replacing it with a new one. Several forensic scientists and chemists who studied the wall in recent years have been unable to come up with a reasonable explanation for the hand-print that can be traced back to 1877.

The West Nickel Mines School Shooting

Sadly, we have become almost numb to the increasing violence everyday in our country. But the events of October 2, 2006, shocked even the most jaded observer—first, because the victims were children and second, because it happened to the Amish, a community that makes a conscious decision to insulate itself from the modern world. Charles Carl Roberts, who was not a member of the Amish community, entered a one-room schoolhouse called West Nickel Mines School with three guns. Although he let some people in the schoolhouse leave, he eventually opened fire in the classroom. Three girls were killed, two more died later from their injuries and five girls were injured. Roberts committed suicide before he could be taken into custody.

As incredible as the crime itself was, the events following the crime are even more astonishing. The Amish community sent members to comfort Roberts' wife and three young children the day of the shooting as well as to attend his funeral in the spirit of forgiveness. Although they do not traditionally accept help from either their neighbors or the government, they received such an outpouring of donations from around the country that the community set up a fund to pay for the girls' medical expenses. After demolishing the school building the following week, the community built New Hope School at a different site and in a different style that does not resemble the old school. They also set up a fund for the family of the shooter.

DON'T GET TOO EXCITED

Pennsylvania was founded as a place that would welcome people persecuted for their religious beliefs. Seems they weren't as open-minded about sports—William Penn insisted that the first colonial legislature ban "riotous sports." The ban included foot races, wrestling, cudgels (jousting without horses), cockfights and even the "sport" of card playing. Coincidentally, Penn's favorite sport—horse racing—was deemed non-riotous and was not included in the ban. Penn could continue riding his horses in Philadelphia races—on Race Street, of course. Despite William's worries that sports would encourage gambling and drinking, sports have thrived in Pennsylvania (OK, maybe because of the gambling and drinking). The state now boasts seven professional sports teams.

Philadelphia Phillies (MLB)—Philadelphia
World Series Winners: 1980

Original Name: Worcester Ruby Legs (moved to Philadelphia in 1883)

Mascot: Phantatic

Pittsburgh Pirates (MLB)—Pittsburgh
World Series Winners: 1909, 1925, 1960, 1971, 1979

Original Name: Pittsburgh Alleghenys (1887–90; renamed Pirates after poaching players from other teams, including Philadelphia Phillies)

Mascot: Pirate Parrot

Philadelphia 76ers (NBA)—Philadelphia
NBA Champions: 1967, 1983

Original Name: Warriors (moved to San Francisco in 1963; Syracuse Nationals then moved to Philadelphia and became 76ers)

Mascot: Hip Hop

Philadelphia Eagles (NFL)—Philadelphia
Super Bowl Champions: None

Mascot: Swoop

Fight Song: Pennsylvania Polka

Pittsburgh Steelers (NFL)—Pittsburgh
Super Bowl Champions: 1974, 1975, 1978, 1979, 2005

Original Name: Pittsburgh Pirates (1933–40)

Mascot: Steely McBeam

Philadelphia Flyers (NHL)—Philadelphia
Stanley Cup Champions: 1974, 1975

Original Name: Philadelphia Quakers played for one season, 1930–31. When hockey returned to Philadelphia in 1967, the team was called the Philadelphia Flyers.

Mascot: Slapshot (1976 season only); they occasionally "borrow" Phlex—the mascot for the Philadelphia Phantoms, a minor league hockey team

Pittsburgh Penguins (NHL)—Pittsburgh

Stanley Cup Champions: 1991, 1992

Original Name: Pittsburgh Pirates (1925–30). The team moved to Philadelphia and was renamed the Philadelphia Quakers (1930–31). Hockey didn't return to Pittsburgh until 1967, and the team was called the Pittsburgh Penguins.

Mascot: Iceburgh the Penguin

DID YOU KNOW?

The colors of the three diamonds in the Pittsburgh Steelers logo were not chosen randomly. Red symbolizes ore, yellow symbolizes coal and blue symbolizes steel.

PHENOMENAL PENNSYLVANIA

For the 1943 season, the Eagles and the Steelers played as one team—the Steagles (also known as Phil-Pitt). Athletes were enlisting or being drafted because of World War II, and neither football team had enough players to play individually. The team played in both Philadelphia and Pittsburgh and finished 5-4-1.

Pennsylvania's Most Successful Team

When the American League was created in 1901, a second Philadelphia baseball team joined the roster—the Philadelphia Athletics. You might know them better as the Kansas City A's, where they played from 1954 to 1968 or the Oakland A's, where they've played ever since. But in their 53 years at Philadelphia, the Athletics contributed quite a few athletes and records to the history of baseball. They won the World Series in 1910, 1911, 1913, 1929 and 1930. Baseball greats including Shoeless Joe Jackson, Ty Cobb, Connie Mack and Eddie Plank all played

with the A's. Five Philly A's were named MVP: Eddie Collins Sr. in 1914, Mickey Cochrane in 1928, Lefty Grove in 1931, Jimmie Foxx in 1932 and 1933, and Bobby Shantz in 1952.

Born to Play

"Sir, you are the greatest athlete in the world." What do you reply when King Gustav V of Sweden says that to you? If you're Jim Thorpe and you've just won Olympic gold, "Thanks, King" is enough. Although Thorpe was born in Oklahoma as a member of the Sauk and Fox tribes, it was Pennsylvania that welcomed him twice—once as a young boy to attend the Carlisle Industrial Indian School and then again after his death when Oklahoma said "No thanks" to what they felt was an athletic king in disgrace.

When he wasn't learning a trade at Carlisle, James Francis Thorpe, who was given the Indian name of Wa-Tho-Huk or "Bright Path," was learning how to play ball from Coach Glen Scobie "Pop" Warner. As a halfback at Carlisle, Thorpe came up against Dwight Eisenhower—Army's halfback—in 1912. After beating teams such as Army and Harvard, the Carlisle Industrial

Indian School team became national collegiate champions. At age 24, Thorpe participated in the 1912 Olympics in Antwerp, Belgium. He came home with double gold in both decathlon and pentathlon and broke longstanding records. Thorpe was barely back on U.S. soil before the Olympic committee decided that two semi-professional seasons of baseball that paid $15 a week made Thorpe a professional athlete. They stripped him of his medals and took an eraser to the record books.

Thorpe didn't let the snotty Olympic committee sour him on sports. He played baseball for the New York Giants, Cincinnati Reds and Boston Braves. But he didn't overlook football, playing and coaching for the Canton Ohio Bulldogs, Cleveland Indians, Oorang Indians and Chicago Cardinals and serving as first President of the NFL. When Thorpe, a California resident, died in 1953, his family wanted to bring him home to Oklahoma and build a memorial for him and his many accomplishments. Oklahoma, embarrassed by the whole stripped-of-his-Olympic-medals incident, wasn't interested in bringing a scandal home.

Even though he never visited in his lifetime, the Pennsylvania towns of Mauch Chunk and East Mauch Chunk merged to form the community of Jim Thorpe and offer one of the world's greatest athletes a resting place with King Gustav's words carved into his red granite memorial. Thorpe was inducted into the Football Hall of Fame in 1963. And as for the scandal that Oklahoma wanted no part of? In 1982, the Olympic Committee reversed their decision and restored Thorpe's medals and records.

It's Just College Football....

Someone said that in Pennsylvania—once. Thanks to JoePa (he has only one name—like Madonna), head coach of the Penn State Nittany Lions, college football has become the official state hobby. Every Saturday, thousands of fanatics (fans, I meant fans) pour into Happy Valley wearing their white and blue. Sure they come to watch the plays, fumbles and touchdowns, but

they also come to get a glimpse of the little guy on the sidelines with his thick, black-rimmed glasses and his high-water pants. Playing quarterback and cornerback at Brown University was just a warm-up for Joe Paterno from Brooklyn. He joined Penn State after graduation as assistant coach under Rip Engle before becoming head coach in 1966. And that was when Penn State football became PENN STATE FOOTBALL. What more can you say about Joe Paterno? How about...

☛ five undefeated seasons

☛ more bowl wins that any college coach in history

☛ more wins than any college coach in history

☛ longest run as a college coach with one team

☛ entered the College Football Hall of Fame in 2006

The name on the front of the jersey is what really matters, not the name on the back.

—Joe Paterno

Gentlemen, Start your Engines...

Pennsylvania boys seem to have a talent for driving fast and getting into trouble. Is it any surprise that Pennsylvania weekends have a soundtrack of motors revving? Race cars speed around more than 50 race tracks spread out across the state. But when Pennsylvania race fans don't feel like traveling to their local dirt track to see a hometown boy take the flag, they can just switch on the TV. Plenty of Pennsylvania racers have made it to the Big Show.

Racing seems to run in families, and one Lehigh Valley family that NASCAR and Indy fans have been enjoying for half a century has been the Andretti family. Twin brothers Mario and Aldo began the racing tradition in 1959. Unfortunately, after serious crashes in 1959 and 1960, Aldo gave up racing. But he was eventually replaced by his son John. Mario's sons Michael and Jeff and daughter Barbara Dee were also drawn to the track. Barbara Dee raced dirt bikes during her childhood but grew up to become a singer and songwriter. For her brothers, the lure was checkered flags, not Grammy awards.

The Andretti family set a record in 1992 when they had four family members—Mario, Michael, Jeff and John—in the Indianapolis 500. One year earlier, the family set the record for having the most members named rookie of the year—Mario

(1965), Michael (1984) and Jeff (1991). The family broke their own record in 2006 when Michael's son Marco also captured the title. We can hardly wait to see what the fourth generation of Andrettis will bring to racing.

Pennsylvania Players

Joe Amato (racer)

Kobe Bryant (basketball)

Wilt Chamberlain (basketball)

Ed Collins (baseball)

Mike Ditka (football)

Reggie Jackson (baseball)

Betsy King (golf)

Dan Marino (football)

Joe Montana (football)

Stan Musial (baseball)

Joe Namath (football)

Arnold Palmer (golf)

Jimmy Spenser (racer)

Johnny Unitas (football)

Sports Milestones

The first World Series was held in Pittsburgh in 1903. The Boston Pilgrims beat the Pittsburgh Pirates five games to three. Despite their team's defeat, Pittsburgh baseball fans built Forbes Field, the first baseball stadium, in 1909.

The Schuylkill Navy, the nation's oldest amateur athletic group, was founded in 1858. In case you haven't guessed, the Navy is a group that rows racing shells. Thanks to the Navy, it looks like Christmas all year long along the Schuylkill River, where 10 Victorian boathouses are outlined in lights and brighten up the skyline.

Tarzan may have ended up in the jungle, but he started out in Windber. Along the way, Johnny Weissmuller won 67 world records, as well as five gold medals in the 1924 and 1928 Olympics. Then Hollywood called, and Johnny put his swimming skills to use portraying Tarzan in 12 movies.

We've had arena football since 1889, when the first indoor football game was played—on the parquet floor of the Academy of Music. Symphony fans were appalled! Football fans moved outdoors for the first night football game played under lights at Mansfield in 1892.

Ed Walsh, born in Plains, was known for having the best spitball in the league (back when spitballs were still legal). Walsh played from 1904 until 1917, with his greatest season being 1908 with the White Sox when his earned run average (ERA)—or mean earned runs given up by the pitcher for every nine innings pitched—was only 1.42. Walsh once estimated he used his spitter 90 percent of the time. That's a lot of spit, Ed!

Penn's Relays was started in 1895 at the University of Pennsylvania in Philadelphia. The three-day event is the largest and longest-running track and field event, with an average of 20,000 athletes of all ages competing.

The first African-American quarterback was Willie Thrower of New Kensington. After Thrower's 1953 stint with the Chicago Bears, it was 15 years before another African-American quarterback took to the field.

Not every horse you see grazing in a Pennsylvania meadow spends his workdays pulling a farmer's plow. The state boasts several Kentucky Derby winners including Barbaro (2006), Smarty Jones (2004) and Lil E. Tee (1992).

The first recorded billiard match was held in Philadelphia in 1858. Unfortunately, visiting Englishman Michael Phelan won the $1000 against local favorite Ralph Benjamin.

It was 1892 and the Allegheny Athletics Association really wanted to win their upcoming football game against the Pittsburgh Athletic Club. Hoping to stack the deck, they paid Yalie Pudge Heffelfinger $500 to join the team. And the first professional football player was born! Baseball had gone pro three decades earlier when the Philadelphia A's hired Alfred J. Reach to play for $25 a week.

He may not have been an athlete, but Stephen Foster of Towanda and Athens wrote a famous sporting song we all know—"Camptown Races." In 1948, a short movie *Camptown Races* illustrated the 1850 song. The race has changed a bit since Foster penned his lyrics—the race is actually 6.1 miles (not five), racers go from Camptown to Merryall (not around a track) and the competitors aren't bob-tailed nags but men and women.

Ora Washington of Germantown may have been one of the greatest female athletes of the 20th century. Never heard of her? Probably because she was trapped behind the color barrier. Washington earned eight singles titles on the American Tennis Association between 1929 and 1937. She was also an Olympic track star in 1930, a player and coach for the Philadelphia Tribunes basketball team between 1932 and 1942 and a professional golfer in the '40s and '50s. The second-class status given to African American athletes at the time is best illustrated by what this great athlete did to supplement her meager income from playing in African-American leagues—she was a domestic. Instead of doing product endorsements, Ora was using the products in her job as a maid for a wealthy Main Line family.

In 1925, the Pottsville Maroons had a record of 9–2, and the Chicago Cardinals were 9–1. Because the teams hadn't met yet, a game was arranged, and the Maroons won the game, which was billed "the NFL Championship." When the Maroons played an exhibition game against the Notre Dame All-Stars in Philadelphia a few weeks later, they were penalized for playing out of their territory and stripped of their title. But not according to Pennsylvanians who will still tell you, "We wuz robbed!"

Philadelphia's Wilt Chamberlain set a record that still stands today—and seems unbeatable. In the 1962 season, Chamberlain was averaging 50.4 points per game, but it was during a game pitting his Philadelphia Warriors against the New York Knicks that he became the first player to score 100 points in one game. Another Philadelphian, Kobe Bryant came closest to breaking the record when he scored 81 points for the LA Lakers against Toronto in 2006.

You can't tell the players without a program—and before 1913, you couldn't even with one. Players' jerseys were identical until Penn became the first team to wear jerseys with numbers on the back when they played against the University of Wisconsin during the 1913 football season.

Take Me Out to the Ballgame

For many boys and girls, their first taste of baseball is Little League, and for that they have a Pennsylvania native to thank. When young Harold "Major" and Jimmy Gehron of Williamsport wanted to play a little baseball, they could always count on their Uncle Tuck to pitch a few balls and retrieve the wild hits. But after twisting his ankle on a lilac bush while chasing a ball, Uncle Tuck—better known outside the family as Carl Stotz— began to wonder if it would be more fun for the boys (and less tiring for him) if they had a regular team. In 1939, he organized three teams: Lycoming Dairy, Lundy Lumber and Jumbo Pretzel, with his nephews as teammates on Lycoming Dairy. By 1946, the league included 12 Pennsylvania teams.

The league was making news but so were some ex-players. In 1947 the first Little Leaguer was drafted by a professional baseball team. Allen "Sonny" Yearick, a former player for the original 1939 Little League teams, was picked up by the Boston Braves. That same year, Little League teams began springing up outside Pennsylvania—and eventually outside the country. The league now has more than 200,000 teams in all 50 states and in more than 80 countries. The organization is the same today as it was when it was founded—the coaches, local organizers and field workers are all volunteers. Incredibly, an organization that allows 2.8 million children throughout the world to play baseball each spring has approximately 110 paid employees.

Even Benchwarmers can be Hall of Famers

The Little League World Series, first held in 1947 with 11 teams competing, continues to be held in Williamsport. Williamsport is also home to the Peter J. McGovern Little League Museum Hall of Fame. Although, like all sports halls of fame, it displays the history of the sport, the milestones that were reached and the sport's greatest athletes, it also celebrates those who have, in the words of the Little League Pledge, kept the promise to "always do my best." Not all of the former Little Leaguers now enshrined in the Hall Of Excellence were outstanding athletes—but they were outstanding people. Some inductees into the Hall of Excellence include police officers, firefighters, educators, doctors, politicians, military personnel, lawyers, business owners, actors, singers, astronauts, engineers and authors.

President George Bush, Tom Selleck, George Will, Dave Barry, Bruce Springsteen, Kevin Costner, General Peter Pace and Detective Nancy dos Reis can all include Little Leaguer on their resume. Athletes such as Dusty Baker, Pierre Turgeon, Krissy Wendell, Cathy Gerring, Brian Sipe, Dan O'Brien, Jim Palmer and Kareem Abdul-Jabbar have taken the foundation they received in Little League and built careers as pro athletes or competed in the Olympics. And all because Carl Stotz sprained his ankle.

HOMEGROWN GOODIES

From Peanuts to Millions

Despite his dapper top hat, cane and spats Mr. Peanut is a Pennsylvania boy. Amedeo Obici came to Wilkes-Barre via Italy when he was just 11 years old. He might have been just one of a hundred other immigrant fruit vendors if he hadn't bought himself a peanut roaster. He developed a better way to roast peanuts, became known as the "Peanut Specialist" and by the time he was 30 years old was co-founder of Planters Peanut and Chocolate Company. "Born" in 1916 as a publicity contest, Mr. Peanut helps sell about $600 million of nut products annually.

It's Cookie Time

In 1933, a Girl Scout troop held a baking demonstration in the window of the Philadelphia Gas and Electric Company. Demand was so great that the next year they hired a local bakery to bake trefoil-shaped cookies, which they sold for the bargain price of 23 cents a box or six boxes for $1.35. Cookie sales had finally taken the leap from homemade bake sales to big business. Girl Scouts now sell over 200 million boxes a year.

Lunch Can-Ready Dessert

Once upon a time, grocers would buy cakes from bakeries and, when the baked goods arrived at their store, grocers sliced, wrapped and sold them. In 1913, Philip Bauer and Herbert Morris decided they'd be the grocers' favorite bakery if they could deliver baked goods that were already sliced and wrapped. They were right—grocers (and cake lovers) couldn't get enough of the Tastycakes, which sold for a dime a piece.

Bubbles of Fun

Some accountants play golf on their days off; others chase beautiful women. Walter Diemer invented bubble gum—which worked out well because Monday through Friday he worked in the accounting department of the Fleer Chewing Gum Company in Philadelphia. Soon the 23-year-old was teaching salesmen how to blow bubbles for demonstrations while other accountants counted the $1.5 million dollars Double Bubble made the first year it was produced—1928. Diemer always insisted with a shrug, "It was an accident. I was doing something else and ended up with bubbles."

DID YOU  KNOW?

Most bubble gum is pink because when Walter Diemer was inventing it, pink was the only food coloring in the factory.

Who Has Time to Mix Their Own Soda?

For years, people made root beer from herbs they gathered. Then Charles Hires, a Philadelphia druggist, got married. On his honeymoon, he tasted a delicious root beer made by a local woman and obtained her recipe. First, he sold only the packaged herbs, which had to be brewed at home with water, but eventually he mixed the herbs with carbonated water for a little fizz. By 1893, he was selling Hires Root Beer, the first commercially bottled root beer.

One Scoop or Two?

Over half a million cows call Pennsylvania home—the human population of Pittsburgh is only 325,337. So what are all those cows doing besides chewing their cud? Making milk to the tune of 10.8 billion pounds (between 1,227,272,727 and 1,270,588,235 gallons) of milk a year. Pennsylvania's top industry is agriculture, and the biggest chunk of that is dairy. Cheese, yogurt, sour cream…enough about that boring stuff. Let's talk

about ice cream—56 million gallons of ice cream a year. Through the years, Pennsylvania has made ice cream history more than once.

1843—Nancy Johnson of Philadelphia patented an "artificial freezer" that helped make the large-scale manufacture of ice cream possible.

1866—William Breyer started Breyer's Ice Cream with a hand-crank machine in his Philadelphia kitchen. His first customers were his neighbors. The company now sells 1.2 billion dollars worth of frozen treats a year. They no longer use the hand crank machine.

1874—Robert M. Green's treat of carbonated water, cream and syrup was selling just fine at the 50th Anniversary of the Franklin Institute, until he ran out of cream. He substituted ice cream, hoping his customers wouldn't notice. But they did—and so did Mr. Green's wallet. Instead of $6, the inventor of the ice cream soda quickly made $600. Quite a haul for one day!

1904—Dr. William Strickler was an apprentice pharmacist at Tassel Pharmacy in Latrobe when he came up with a new ice cream treat: three scoops of ice cream topped with pineapple, strawberry and chocolate sauces, a dollop of whipped cream, chopped nuts and a cherry. And don't forget the banana—sliced along its length. His banana split was a whooping 10 cents, twice the cost of a regular sundae.

1905—Maybe you saw this one coming…Pennsylvania is also home to the first manufacturer of "banana boat" dishes. That's how Dr. Strickler described them when he put in an order to the Westmoreland Glass Company of nearby Grapeville the year after he invented the banana split. Dr. Strickler was charged $1.50 for a dozen dishes

1909—Leonard L. Westling of Pittsburgh patented the Edible Cone Shaper.

1918—Albert George and family bought a few used cone baking machines and started the George & Thomas Cone Company in Hermitage. After a few years, happy with their success, the owners changed their name to the more familiar Joy Cone Company.

Almost a century later, the family is the largest supplier of cones in the world—1.5 billion a year.

1930s—Founded in 1894 by Jacob Hershey (no relation to the Hershey of chocolate fame), Hershey's Ice Cream became the first manufacturer to offer pre-packaged pints and half gallons of ice cream for "takeout."

1959—Bassett's Ice Cream, known for unusual flavors, produced 50 tubs of borscht sherbet at the request of Soviet Premier Nikita Krushchev.

1986—Ian Cooper, a dental supply salesman, had an ice cream in one hand and a pretzel stick in the other when he asked himself (actually, he asked his neighbor and customer Steve Sunshine, who was also enjoying an ice cream at the time), "Wouldn't it be great if there was a pretzel cone?" When Ian and Steve became The Cone Guys and introduced the world to pretzel cones, many people agreed—pretzel cones are great.

THE LAND OF PRETZELS

Asleep on the Job

Contrary to what your boss might say, sometimes it does pay to nap at work. In the 1600s, an anonymous apprentice in a Pennsylvania bakery fell asleep next to his oven one day and left his pretzels in a bit too long. Since their invention by an Italian monk in 610, all pretzels had been soft. That is, until the day of the sleepy baker. The master baker was furious and, before firing the shiftless apprentice, he bit into one of those sorry, dried up excuses for a pretzel. He liked it—and the apprentice lived to bake another day.

What an Unusual Tip!

Julius Sturgis, a Lititz baker, was the first one to open a commercial pretzel bakery. Rumor has it that a transient stopped by the bakery in 1860 looking for a job. There were no job openings, but Sturgis did invite him home for dinner. As a thank you, the out-of-work baker passed on an old family pretzel recipe. Sturgis didn't have any experience with pretzel baking so he decided to test the first batch on his wife and 14 children They must have given it the thumbs up—by the next year, neighbors in need of bread had to visit another bakery because Sturgis had switched to strictly pretzels. He delivered them daily to local taverns packed in huge barrels—leading the way for Pennsylvania to become the pretzel capital.

Where Pretzels Are King

For 75 years, pretzels were twisted by hand—even the fastest twister could only make 40 pretzels a minute. Thank goodness for the Reading Pretzel Machinery Company—it introduced automatic pretzel twisting machines that could make 245 pretzels per minute, or 5 tons a day. Sound like a lot of pretzels? Not really, considering that $561 million pretzels are sold each year and 80 percent are made in Pennsylvania. And quite a few stay in Pennsylvania—the average American eats 1.5 to 2 pounds of pretzels a year. The average Pennsylvanian? Twelve pounds! How could any one eat that many pretzels? Easy if you're from the state that dozens of pretzels manufacturers call home. You could eat a different pretzel each day for a year and still not taste all that "Pretzelvania" has to offer: hard, soft, thin, fat, twists, rods, nuggets, baldies, buggy-shaped, star-shaped, circles, sour dough, organic, jalapeño, honey mustard, hot buffalo wing, cheese, butter, wheat, cinnamon, oat, peanut butter filled, chocolate covered …a pretzel bonanza.

Pennsylvania Pretzels

Aunt Annie's Hand Rolled Soft Pretzels—Annie Beiler started selling pretzels at farmer's markets to help fund her family's dream of a free family-counseling center in their hometown of Lancaster. The company now sells pretzels in 15 different countries.

Benzel's Pretzels—the family owned bakery still uses the recipe Adolph Benzel brought with him when he immigrated to the U.S. from Germany in 1911.

Hammond's Pretzel Bakery—the Hammond family has been making pretzels since the 1800s. The fourth and fifth generations now run the factory.

Intercourse Pretzel House—want to spell your name with pretzels? Intercourse sells letter-shaped pretzels.

Julius Sturgis Pretzel House—pretzel lovers can still visit the original Julius Sturgis Pretzel bakery and learn how to hand twist a pretzel. Be prepared, it isn't as easy as you'd think.

Martin's Bakery—Martin's is run by a Mennonite family that hires local Mennonite women as pretzel twisters. Visiting the twisting room is like traveling back in time—the women wear modest dresses and prayer caps and often sing hymns as they work.

Revonah Pretzels—did you guess? Renovah got its name by twisting its hometown's name—Hanover.

Snyder's of Hanover—look to Snyder's for some original flavored pretzels such as pumpernickel, sesame, garlic bread and honey mustard.

Tom Sturgis Pretzels—Julius Sturgis' grandson Marriot "Tom" Sturgis moved to Reading, where he opened his own pretzel bakery.

Uncle Henry's Handmade Pretzels—their motto— "Dee Grummer Dinger Sin Wunderbore Gute." Don't speak Pennsylvania Dutch? "These Crooked Things Are Wonderful Good."

Unique Pretzel Bakery—the Henry family had been making pretzels for over 50 years when a mistake produced a new pretzel in the 1950s. Soon this craggy, crunchy pretzel, called the split, was the only kind they were making.

Wege Pretzel Company—weeg? Weg? Weg-ee? Actually it's pronounced wig-gie.

MADE IN PENNSYLVANIA...

That's My Kind of Trail

Pennsylvania doesn't just make pretzels. It is home to all sorts of snack foods. In fact, you could work your way through the state following the Snack Food Trail. Naturally, you'd have to start out in York, where you could enjoy Stauffer's cookies, especially their animal crackers. York is also home to Bickel's Snack Foods—potato chips, corn chips, cheese curls, pork rinds and more. From there it's a quick hop to Hanover and Utz Snack Foods. If you love crunchy snack food, make another stop at Herr's in Nottingham and don't pass up their kettle cooked potato chips. Ready for dessert? Bethlehem's Just Born (don't you just love that name?) serves up jelly beans and other chewy

candies. They also make the nests for those sticky, sweet treats—
Marshmallow Peeps ®. If you have any room left you can visit
Altoona, where Boyer Candy specializes in "cup" candies—not
only peanut butter cups, like another candy giant, but peanut
butter coated in butterscotch, and marshmallow covered with
chocolate and coconut. And eating isn't the only fun—most of
these companies also offer free factory tours where you can
watch millions and millions of delicious snacks be made.

ALL THINGS HERSHEY

Mmmmm...Chocolate...

If you haven't heard the name Hershey, you've never stared at the assortment of candy bars tempting you as you stand in line at the grocery store. But when you're from Pennsylvania, you know that Hershey is much more than the name of a chocolate company. When Pennsylvanians hear Hershey, they don't just think candy; they think roller coasters, roses, orphans, street lights, Native Americans and a host of other things.

The Man

Before there was Hershey's Chocolate, there was Milton Snavely Hershey. Milton wasn't a great businessman and had not one, not two, but three candy companies go under before he finally started the Lancaster Candy Company in 1883. When he saw German chocolate making equipment at the World's Columbian Exposition a decade later, he decided to coat his caramels with milk chocolate. When he learned that people were buying his chocolate-coated caramels, licking off the chocolate and tossing the caramel centers into the trash, he decided his fortune was in chocolate. He returned to his hometown of Derry Church, where local farmers could supply him with plenty of fresh milk for his milk chocolate. Sadly, Milton and his wife Catherine never had children to share their tremendous success with. But when Milton died in 1945 at age 88, he left a legacy that affected millions of people—and not just by selling them chocolate.

The Company

By 1900, Milton was able to produce an affordable milk chocolate bar, a treat that had always been a luxury of the rich. By 1907, the company had developed a product recognizable throughout the world—the Hershey Kiss. Some say it was named after the smooching sound the machinery made as it produced the kisses. The company rallied to meet all crises: they made chocolate bars for World War I soldiers, developed new products so employees wouldn't be laid off during the Depression and provided more than a billion Ration D bars that wouldn't melt in hot weather for World War II. Milton was always adding new products to the company but missed out when one of his foremen came to him with a great idea—peanut butter coated with milk chocolate. Even though Milton didn't think it was a good idea, he loaned Harry Burnett Reese money to start his own business. Forty years later, the Reese family had the last laugh when they sold the H.B. Reese Candy Company to Hershey for $23.5 million dollars. Milton may have known chocolate, but Harry knew his peanut butter.

The Town

Hershey may be the only town in the United States that screams chocolate. Not only are the streetlights shaped like Hershey Kisses, but if you open your window at the right time (3PM, according to most residents) you can inhale chocolate breezes— try staying on your diet in that kind of environment! The man that built what was basically a "company town" for his employees wasn't interested in cheap row homes and a company store. Milton Hershey wanted to build a dream town with quality homes, schools and even a park (which eventually became the amusement park, Hersheypark). During the Great Depression when families all over the country were abandoning their hometowns in their search for work, Hershey's company town became a magnet for those in need of work. Hershey initiated a "Great Building Campaign," building projects designed to keep people in work, such as a theatre, sports arena, stadium and hotel. Milton and his wife Catherine were each collectors—tendencies that benefited the entire town. Catherine's love of roses eventually became the Hershey Gardens, and his interest in local history became the Hershey Museum.

The School

Both the Hersheys loved children, which led to their establishing the Hershey Industrial School (later renamed the Milton Hershey School). Although the school was originally for orphaned boys, over the years girls and disadvantaged children who had living parents were admitted to the boarding school, where children lived in small group homes overseen by married houseparents during the school year. In 1918, Hershey transferred most of his personal wealth into a trust for the school to aid in expansion. Today there are approximately 1700 students at the school and 8000 alumni throughout the world. The school even awards scholarships to students after high school graduation so they can attend college.

DID YOU  KNOW?

Milton Hershey bought a ticket on the *Titanic* but had to return to the United States earlier so he booked passage on the *Amerika* instead. Just think, if he had gone down with the ship in 1912, we would not have the delicious treats he created, not to mention his school, garden, amusement park, theatre and more.

More Pennsylvania Chocolate

Asher's Chocolates—the oldest continuously family owned and operated candy company is led by the fourth generation of Ashers. Although the factory moved to Souderton, each morning a van travels the 25 miles from the original neighborhood, Germantown, to the new factory, bringing experienced candy makers to work.

Daffin's Candies—the family owned company in Sharon is known for its Chocolate Kingdom, which includes creatures such as a 400-pound chocolate turtle, a 125-pound chocolate reindeer and a 75-pound chocolate frog.

Gardners Candies—James "Pike" Gardner, founder of Gardeners Candies in 1897, added a special twist when he began traveling with a horse and wagon to fairs and carnivals around Tyrone, selling his sweets.

Sherm Edwards Candies—where else can you nibble on chocolate covered pickles?

Wilbur Chocolates—Henry Oscar Wilbur was the owner of a successful hardware and stove business but something sweeter beckoned to him—chocolate.

Wolfgang Candy—Wolfgang Candy wasn't satisfied with chocolate covered strawberries—their chocolate covered blueberries, cranberries and raspberries are a big hit in the U.S. and Japan.

REGIONAL DELIGHTS

Does It Taste Better Than It Sounds?

The Food Network has a show in which a host with an iron stomach goes around the world eating delicacies most of us wouldn't consider food. Like flies. Not a regular on your weekly grocery list? Maybe you haven't been hanging around in the right places. In Pennsylvania, the great debate isn't "Would you eat fly pie?" but "Do you like wet bottom or dry bottom fly pie?" Before you line up The Food Network for a trip to PA…it isn't actually fly pie. This Pennsylvania Dutch dessert is called Shoofly Pie. Most pie lovers will tell you it's because this molasses pie is so sweet you have to shoo the flies away from it. Others (people who have too much time on their hands, in our opinion) will tell you that shoofly pie is named after cauliflower (seriously). Seems the French name for cauliflower is "choufleur" and the crumb topping of shoofly pie resembles a cauliflower. According to this theory, French immigrants would ask their Pennsylvania Dutch neighbors for a slice of their "choufleur" pie and the French moniker became Dutchified to "shoofly." Yes, we find it hard to believe, too. Still wondering about the wet bottom vs. dry bottom debate? Wet bottom is a gooey molasses layer, whereas dry bottom is a crumb cake type bottom, more like your traditional apple or peach pie. You can try both, but if you're looking for a gooey, sweet pie, don't you want to go whole hog? Wet bottom rules!

Try It. You'll Like It.

Although the Pennsylvania Dutch are renowned for their great cooking, the names of the dishes sometimes make a hungry visitor think twice. Perhaps it was an unwillingness to let anything go to waste that led to green tomato pie, fried green tomatoes, and dandelion salad with hot bacon dressing (not the yellow flowers, just the early green leaves). Not interested in eating weeds? Try pepper cabbage (heavy on the cabbage, light on the pepper) or red beet eggs (picture a hard boiled egg—but pink). Chow-chow doesn't involve furry dogs but lots of vegetables cut into small pieces, jarred and pickled. On the Tuesday before Lent, some people celebrate with Carnival or Mardi Gras. Pennsylvania has a more low key celebration—Faschnacht Day. *Faschnachts* are holeless donuts designed to use up all the lard that one is not supposed to eat during Lent, a time of sacrifice. If you get over the odd idea of a donut with potatoes in it, you'll discover that it makes a delicious dessert. While you're having dessert, don't forget whoopie pie. Actually it's more like a cookie sandwich—two large soft chocolate cookies with a white fluffy center. Apple butter, *schnitz und knepp* (apples and dumplings), chicken pot pie, fritters, dumplings, sand tarts, funnel cakes, hog maw (stuffed pig's stomach), cottage cheese pie, sauerkraut…why are there only three meals a day?

DID YOU  KNOW?

In South Philly when you want a little more spaghetti sauce on your pasta, ask for more gravy.

57—The Magic Number

Some foods—such as scrapple—are unique to one spot. Others are everywhere—such as one that is found in 97 percent of American households and in three out of four restaurants. That's right, that ever-popular condiment (which could be soup in a pinch)—ketchup. Who doesn't have ketchup in their kitchen? And chances are, if you have ketchup in your kitchen, you've got a little piece of Pennsylvania. Henry J. "Harry" Heinz didn't start one of the world's most recognizable companies with ketchup. Instead, Harry burst on the Sharpsburg scene (on the outskirts of Pittsburgh) in 1869 with his mother's horseradish. His big selling point? He put his horseradish in clear jars, not the traditional green glass ones, so picky housewives could examine it and make sure he wasn't packing it with fillers such as turnips, leaves or sawdust. (Yuck! No wonder these ladies didn't want to buy ready-made horseradish). Honest Harry did so well, he soon added pickles, relish, sauerkraut, and vinegar to his company's offerings. The Panic of 1873 forced Harry into bankruptcy in 1875, but he came back the same year—with ketchup. He kept adding new products: red and green pepper sauce, cider vinegar, apple butter, chili sauce, mincemeat, mustard, tomato soup, olives, pickled onions, pickled cauliflower, baked beans and the first sweet pickles. It wasn't until 1896 that he reached that magical number: 57 varieties. There's no special meaning behind that number—he just picked it out of the air.

Why were Heinz's products such a big hit? After all, when he started his company, any housewife worth her weight knew how to make all these foods. Sure, but making them was a big pain in the...well you get the idea. Housewives jumped at the chance to buy ready made, and before you knew it, old family recipes were lost and young housewives had no idea how to whip up a good batch of mustard. And besides, the Heinz stuff was just as good as homemade. At least husbands weren't complaining. Heinz not only filled that old business axiom "Find a need and fill it," he went one better. With his convenient products, he didn't just find a need—he created one. Sneaky, Harry.

> *To do a common thing uncommonly well brings success.*
> –Henry John Heinz, Founder of Heinz Company

During World War II, the H.J. Heinz Company produced many products necessary for the war effort (have you ever tried to swallow powdered eggs without ketchup?). Actually, their specialty was glider wings for the Allied invasion of Europe.

Home of the Cheesesteak

Of course it's impossible to go to Philadelphia and not eat a cheesesteak—it's a law. OK, it's not a law. The only thing that'll happen if you visit Philadelphia and don't eat a cheesesteak is

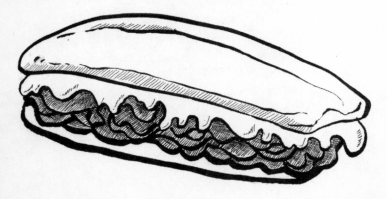

that you will become infamous. Strangers on the street will point at you and laugh. Your own family will refer to your cheesesteak-free visit as "The Unfortunate Incident." It's almost impossible to visit Philly and not have a cheesesteak simply because they are everywhere. Cheesesteak vendors are to Philly what coffee houses are to Seattle.

Swiss Cheese? Never Heard of It

Real cheesesteaks have few variations. They are long Italian rolls made at Vilotti-Pisanelli or Amoroso's Baking Company, filled with thinly sliced and fried steak. These rolls are one of the reasons that many experts claim true Philly cheesesteaks can only be found in Philadelphia. You can choose a sandwich with fried onions (wit) or not (wit out). You can also choose to have it topped with Cheese Whiz (wiz) or not (no wiz). Some cheesesteak places will tolerate American or provolone cheese as well as a few other additions: fried peppers, fried mushrooms, mozzarella or pizza sauce. But the further you stray from the three basics: steak, Cheese Whiz and onions, the faster you brand yourself as an outsider. The Philadelphia Daily News reported that, while campaigning for president in 2004, John Kerry ordered Swiss Cheese on his sandwich—the press laughed. Perhaps it was the Swiss Cheese that cost him the election. We'll never know.

Follow the Rules

If you're going to visit the birthplace of the cheesesteak, you'd might as well get the best—and for most cheesesteak aficionados, that means either Pat's or Geno's. In fact, you could do your own little taste test because the two oldest, most famous cheesesteak joints are across the street from each other on Passyunk Avenue near 9th Street in south Philly's Italian Market. Unlike five star restaurants where servers want to tempt you with detailed descriptions of the daily special, the people at cheesesteak joints don't want to converse. You are instructed (sometimes by very specific step-by-step signs) to order in as few words as possible—wiz wit (Cheese Whiz and onions), Provo wit out (Provolone Cheese and no onions). If you insist on getting fancy—peppers, mushrooms, pizza sauce, etc., these deviations often have a number. Do not ask idiotic questions such as what the server recommends or if the grease is drained off the meat. They will only look at you in silent annoyance before shouting "Next!" And then you'd miss out on the best lunch in town—if not the world.

DID YOU KNOW?

Another Pennsylvania sandwich on an Italian roll is the hoagie. During World War I, immigrants worked at the shipyards on Hog Island. The men who worked in the shipyards were called Hoggies, and their lunch cans usually contained a long Italian roll filled with cheese and lunch meats—a hoggy sandwich, eventually shortened to a hoggy. Somewhere in history it became the hoagie (hoe-gee), but it is also know as the sub, po'boy, grinder, hero and—in just a few sections of Pennsylvania and New Jersey—the zep (as in zeppelin).

BETCHA NEVER KNEW...

Pennsylvania has 1.2 million veterans living in the state—fifth highest in the nation. During World War II, more than 1.3 million men and women served in the Armed Forces.

Bessie Wallis Warfield was born in Blue Ridge Summit in 1896. Fast forward to England 1936, when she's Mrs. Simpson. The whole world was shocked when Edward, the future king of England, renounced the crown to marry her. They lived the rest of their lives in France as the Duke and Duchess of Windsor.

The largest city park is 8000-acre Fairmount Park in Philadelphia.

The first auto service station was opened by Gulf Refining Company in Pittsburgh in 1913.

The "Father of Weightlifting" was Bob Hoffman, founder of the York Barbell Company in 1932.

The longest stone arch bridge in the world, with 48 arches, is the 3820-foot Rockville Bridge in Harrisburg

Old Forge has christened itself Pizza Capital of the World. In a town of about 9000 people, they have a pizzeria for every 800 residents. New York City has to survive with one pizzeria for every 2758 residents!

William Boyce, the Chicago newspaper publisher who founded the Boy Scouts in 1910, was born in Plum Boro, Pennsylvania. He married Mary Jean Deacon, a hometown girl who had the nickname "Rattlesnake Jane"—she was an excellent shot and poker player.

Arthur, the young aardvark who has tons of adventures with his friends in books and on the highest rated children's show in TV history, is the creation of Marc Brown, an illustrator that grew up in Erie.

Pennsylvania doesn't like to sell its natural wonders short—Pine Creek Gorge is better known as the Grand Canyon of Pennsylvania, and Bushkill Falls is known as the Niagara Falls of Pennsylvania.

The oldest ethnic festival in the nation is Lithuanian Days, which has been held in Schuylkill County since 1914.

Connellsville, a town of 13,000 people during World War II, opened a free canteen staffed by volunteers for military personnel traveling through town on the B&O Mainline. For two years, the canteen was open 24 hours a day and fed more than 600,000 members of the armed services. That's a lot of sandwiches!

The most valuable baseball card is of a Pittsburgh native, Honus Wagner, or the Flying Dutchman. The American Tobacco Company sponsored the card in 1909 and Honus, a non-smoker, worried that children might buy tobacco while attempting to get his card, so he had it recalled. In 2007, one of his cards sold for $2.8 million.

When the boxer Joe Palooka retired in 1984, the mayor of Wilkes-Barre named a mountain after him, and the town installed a monument. It gets even stranger—Palooka never lived in Wilkes-Barre. So why the hoop-dee-do? Because for almost four decades, the cartoonist Ham Fisher had been telling 50 million readers that his comic strip fighter Joe Palooka was from Wilkes-Barre.

The Frederick and Mary F. Beckley Scholarship gives $1000 away each year to a student at Juanita College in Huntington. The catch? You have to be left-handed.

Pennsylvanians like to stand up and be counted—of the 13 original colonies, Pennsylvania had the most signers of the Declaration of Independence (nine) and the Constitution (eight).

PBS doesn't just stand for public broadcast service—it also stands for the Pennsylvania Bigfoot Society. But don't worry, they aren't looking to mount his (her?) head on the wall—their rules clearly state they are an "observe only" organization.

Lee Iacocca, the man who brought Chrysler back to life, started his life as Lido Anthony Iacocca of Allentown.

After carefully studying the videotape, the Guinness World Record people declared Russell "Rock Bottom" Byers the World Stone Skipping Champ for making a rock skip 51 times on French Creek. The dethroned former champion was also from Pennsylvania—Kurt "Mountain Man" Steiner of Emporium held a record of 40 skips.

With 378 Medals of Honor, Pennsylvanians have received more than 10 percent of the awards. Only New York State has received more Medals of Honor.

TEN REASONS TO LIVE IN PENNSYLVANIA

1. The Rides—Pennsylvania has a dozen amusement parks with a dozen different personalities. Old, new, thrilling, family fun, wet and wild, crazy characters, delicious food, whatever you want, somewhere in the state there's a park for you. When you ride the 1912 Grand Carousel at Knoebels Amusement Resort, you can still grab the brass ring and get a free ride. Dorney Park's Talon is the longest and tallest inverted rollercoaster in the Northeast. Sesame Place has Big Bird. And if you feel like getting romantic, head for Hersheypark where you can smooch your honey 330 feet above ground in the Kissing Tower.

2. Block Parties—They've got lots of different names: block parties, picnics, festivals, fairs, carnivals. Whether they're held on a city street, a rural picnic grounds or in a church basement, people go for one reason—food. Not fast food, not packaged food, not food brought in by a vendor that covers the tri-state area. This is food made by little old ladies in fire company or church kitchens using the secret family recipes their great-grandmothers gave them—bean soup, bleenies, pierogies, cheesesteaks, funnel cakes, halup-kis. Homemade cakes are dropped off by the dozens and sliced into huge pieces by accommodating picnic volunteers. And the food is waiting for you at bargain basement prices, every weekend from Memorial Day until the autumn leaves begin to fall from the trees. Pennsylvania restaurant owners weep when block party season begins.

3. Horse and Buggy Traffic—Being caught behind an Amish horse and buggy with a stoic driver staring straight ahead and cute little kids in their Amish straw hats and bonnets peeking back at you is the perfect traffic jam. Who could

get road rage at somebody wearing suspenders and a bright lime green shirt? The Amish should make us impatient—they're slow on the roads, they talk a little funny and they like to refer to the Bible in everyday conversations. Instead, their attitude is contagious (OK, not the Bible quoting part)—they calm you down. Cardiologists should prescribe a day with the Amish for every one of their patients.

4. Autumn—People pay money to come to our state and look at the trees. Yes, it amazes us. After all, we know what it's like to rake up all those red, yellow and orange leaves once they fall from our trees (or the trees of our neighbor, who never rakes, so his leaves all blow into our yard and we end up…well, you get the picture). But before the raking part, we can sit on our front porch and watch these leaves changing for weeks—for free. Now if we could just get some out-of-staters to come and do the raking.

5. Farmers Markets—Heard of the "buy local" movement? Everyone has, unless they've been locked in the bathroom at McDonald's for a few years. The difference is Pennsylvanians heard about it decades ago when mom packed the family into the station wagon and headed for the farmer's market.

Pennsylvania has a great climate that supports lots of great crops—grapes (and wine), blueberries, watermelons, strawberries, apples, pears, tomatoes, cucumbers, potatoes, mushrooms, lettuce. Want even more local? Try your own yard. Every household in the state has at least one measly tomato plant in a pot on their front porch—most have much more.

6. History—We've got history with a capital "H." Ben Franklin, Gettysburg, Valley Forge...When we say "George Washington slept here," we really mean it. Then there's the fun history: oldest brewery (Yuengling's), oldest golf course (Foxburg), oldest covered bridge (Philadelphia), oldest roller coaster (Lakemont Park) and the first zoo (Philadelphia Zoo).

7. Wildlife—Residents of Pennsylvania cities may have to get their fill of animals at the local zoo, but most state residents just walk into their backyard. Even though they claim to be loners, bears occasionally wander into town to see what humans (and their garbage cans) are up to. And northwest Pennsylvania doesn't call itself Elk Country just for fun. Once you've seen a 1000-pound, elk you don't even notice the 200-pound white-tailed deer that seem to be everywhere—including your vegetable garden. For lovers of ickier things we've got plenty of snakes, salamanders, lizards and frogs. Mornings are more bearable when there's a bird singing outside your bedroom window—and in Pennsylvania, birds are always singing—even on Mondays.

8. Music—How many state citizens could hum a minstrel song from the 1800s? If the state is Pennsylvania and "Oh Dem Golden Slippers"—favorite of the Mummers—is the song, almost everybody. We also do pretty well with polkas, fiddle music and church hymns (remember we were founded for religious freedom). And local bands rock the hosey every weekend. In Pennsylvania we can also claim a variety of favorite sons (and daughters)—the Dorsey Brothers, Dizzy Gillepsie, Bill Halley (and the Comets), Poison, Bobby

Vinton, The Hooters, Dead Milkman, Will Smith (the Fresh Prince), Boyz II Men and Christina Aguilera.

9. Mountains—People who have stood in the shadow of Mount McKinley or Mount Rainey might laugh at our mountains, but what we lack in height we make up for in quantity. It's hard to find a spot in the state where you don't feel as if you are either on top of the world or surrounded on all sides by mountains. Would you expect anything less from a state that has an entire section nicknamed "Endless Mountains"? Pennsylvania mountains give you skiing, hiking and the opportunity to watch about 20,000 raptors (including eagles) follow the Hawk Mountain "highway" when they migrate. And don't forget the waterfalls—including 22 at Rickets Glen State Park alone. In fact, Frank Lloyd Wright built a house, Fallingwater, on top of a waterfall.

10. Waves—There may not be any oceans, but there are plenty of waves in the state. With a few exceptions, Pennsylvania is made up of small towns. To paraphrase the theme song from *Cheers*, "towns where everybody knows your name." And if you're new to the neighborhood, they at least know your car. And after they've seen it in the neighborhood a few times, they start waving when you drive by. Just a quick "Hey, I know you" wave. Pennsylvania neighbors watch your house when you're out of town even if you didn't ask them to; they shovel snow for old ladies; they worry when the ambulance or police car drives down the street; they're proud when they notice your kid's name mentioned in the newspaper for coming in 22nd in a cross-country race. The census bureau would tell you Pennsylvania is made up mostly of small towns, but Pennsylvanians will tell you those small towns are really big families.

ABOUT THE ILLUSTRATORS

Roger Garcia

Roger Garcia is a self-taught artist with some formal training who specializes in cartooning and illustration. He is an immigrant from El Salvador, and during the last few years, his work has been primarily cartoons and editorial illustrations in pen and ink. Recently he has started painting once more. Focusing on simplifying the human form, he uses a bright minimal palette and as few elements as possible. His work can be seen in newspapers, magazines, promo material and on www.rogergarcia.ca

Peter Tyler

Peter is a recent graduate of the Vancouver Film School's Visual Art and Design and Classical animation programs. Though his ultimate passion is in filmmaking, he is also intent on developing his draftsmanship and storytelling, with the aim of using those skills in future filmic misadventures.

Patrick Hénaff

Born in France, Patrick Hénaff is mostly self-taught. He is a versatile artist who has explored a variety of media under many different influences. He now uses primarily pen and ink to draw and then processes the images on computer. He is particularly interested in the narrative power of pictures and tries to use them as a way to tell stories.

Pat Bidwell

Pat has always had a passion for drawing and art. Initially self-taught, Pat completed art studies in visual communication in 1986. Over the years, he has worked both locally and internationally as an illustrator/product designer and graphic designer, collecting many awards for excellence along the way. When not at the drawing board, Pat pursues other interests solo and/or with his wife, Lisa.

ABOUT THE AUTHORS

Jodi M. Webb

Jodi M. Webb came from a practical family where people had "real jobs" and writing was just "a nice little hobby." She obliged her relatives for some time, working as a substitute teacher, bookkeeper, retailer, typist and child caregiver. Jodi wrote articles, but could never fully commit to it. One day while Jodi was working at a donut shop, a regular customer told her "See honey, this is what happens when you don't go to school." It was Independence Day, and Jodi quit. Now Jodi spends her time with her three children, gardening, baking (mainly when she has writer's block) and, of course, writing. She has contributed to art publications, outdoor and parenting magazines and considers herself an eastern seaboard trivia aficionado.

ABOUT THE AUTHORS

Lisa Wojna

Lisa is the co-author of more than a dozen trivia books, as well as being the sole author of nine other non-fiction books. She has worked in the community newspaper industry as a writer and journalist and has traveled all over the world. Although writing and photography have been a central part of her life for as long as she can remember, it's the people behind every story that are her motivation and give her the most fulfilment.

More madcap trivia from Blue Bike Books...

DOG TRIVIA
Humorous, Heartwarming & Amazing
Wendy Pirk

Humans have lived alongside dogs for millennia, but there's more to them than just tail wags, a love for car rides and chasing tennis balls. It is not surprising that there are so many weird facts and fascinating tales about "man's best friend."

Softcover • 5.25" x 8.25" • 208 pages
ISBN13: 978-1-897278-36-9 • ISBN10: 1-897278-36-5 • $14.95

CAT TRIVIA
Humorous, Heartwarming, Weird & Amazing
Diana MacLeod

The most popular pet in North America is mysterious yet companionable, ferocious but cuddly, wild and domestic. Cats fascinate us with their exotic yet familiar ways. For cat lovers, this is a must-have.

Softcover • 5.25" x 8.25" • 224 pages
ISBN13: 978-1-897278-26-0 • ISBN10: 1-897278-26-8 • $14.95

GROSS AND DISGUSTING THINGS ABOUT THE HUMAN BODY
Joanna Emery

The human body may be a wonder of natural engineering, but it can also be pretty gross and bad-smelling. In this fearless little book, find the answers to such profound questions as why are boogers green, why do farts smell and where does belly button lint come from?

Softcover • 5.25" x 8.25" • 224 pages
ISBN13: 978-1-897278-26-0 • ISBN10: 1-897278-25-X • $14.95

Available from your local bookseller or by contacting the distributor,
Lone Pine Publishing • 1-800-518-3541

www.lonepinepublishing.com